Praise for *Hop*

"Finally! A problem-solving book tha[t] ful reflection rather than the pon[d] leave so many of us creative people b[...] problem, a dream unfulfilled, or a life that needs a little extra sparkle, Marney Makridakis's warm, wise, charming book is your golden ticket to a glittering solution. Never underestimate the power of whimsy."
— **SAM BENNETT**, author of *Get It Done!* and founder of
www.TheOrganizedArtistCompany.com

"Are you feeling stuck in manifesting your next creative project? This book is designed to help you get going with it, in wonderfully playful ways. Marney Makridakis provides ideas, exercises, and examples to help you get started, and then to help you finish, your manifestation. She writes again and again, 'just try this.' So open the book and try one of her exercises, just for the fun of it. You may be amazed at what bubbles up."   — **SEENA FROST**, author of *SoulCollage® Evolving*

"Reading and using this book is so much fun that you don't even know you're transforming your life! Marney Makridakis takes the lofty concept of 'manifesting' and breaks it down into simple, clear concepts and effective tools — making it easy and natural to achieve whatever you want to create in your life and experience a world where work feels like play."   — **MARC ALLEN**, author of *The Millionaire Course* and *The Magical Path*

"You know that meaning is important — but do you know how to create it? In her new book *Hop, Skip, Jump*, Marney Makridakis provides exactly the road map you need to lead a more intentional, meaningful life!"   — **ERIC MAISEL**, author of *Life Purpose Boot Camp*

"Inside the colossal play in *Hop, Skip, Jump* is a practicality you won't forget because you had so much fun."
— **JILL BADONSKY**, author of
The Muse Is In: An Owner's Manual to Your Creativity

"I've always marveled at how productive and prolific Marney Makridakis is *and* how she creates with such ease and joy. In her latest book, she unlocks a treasure chest full of playful tools and inspiring right-brain exercises to help us make our wildest dreams come true. Now instead of being jealous of Marney's manifestation superpower, I can hop, skip, jump my way to even more meaning, momentum, and magic in my work and life, and so can you." — **JENNIFER LEE,** author of *The Right-Brain Business Plan*

"Hop, skip, jump with this wonder-full book into changing the way you experience productivity, replacing 'hard work' with conscious play. It's the new route to joy-filled success. If your play-full self longs to achieve practical results, and feel good while doing it, Marney Makridakis shows you exactly how. She has one of the strongest blends of right brain and left brain of anyone I know, and this book is a creative fountain overflowing with her very best tools and techniques."
— **SARK,** author and artist of *Succulent Wild Woman*

"You will have so much fun reading this book that you might not even notice how much you begin to expand the creative capacities in yourself. Yet suddenly you will feel affirmed, alive, and eager to act, and you will hop, skip, jump into a whole new world of very real and powerful possibilities. Marney Makridakis is a sparkling genius."
— **TAMA KIEVES,** *USA Today*–featured visionary career catalyst and bestselling author of *Inspired & Unstoppable: Wildly Succeeding in Your Life's Work!*

"What a truly delightful book. Reading it, I found myself squirming, and I had to jump up and make something. Marney Makridakis offers lively ways to play your way toward a truer life. Such fun."
— **JENNIFER LOUDEN,** teacher and bestselling author of *The Woman's Comfort Book* and *The Life Organizer*

"This book is fun! It is the antidote to workaholism, successomania, and NETD (Never Enough Time Disorder — I made up the disorder part, because I learned in this book that being imaginative is a positive part of play). But seriously — well, as seriously as I can be after immersing myself in all this lightness and delight — after you finish reading it, you'll find work more fulfilling, success more forthcoming, and time on your side."
— **VICTORIA MORAN,** author of *Living a Charmed Life* and *The Good Karma Diet*

Also by Marney K. Makridakis

*Creating Time: Using Creativity
to Reinvent the Clock and Reclaim Your Life*

HOP, SKIP, JUMP

75 Ways to
Playfully Manifest
a Meaningful Life

Marney K. Makridakis

New World Library
Novato, California

 New World Library
14 Pamaron Way
Novato, California 94949

The terms ARTbundance™ and ARTsignments™ are trademarks of Artella Creative Multimedia.

Text design by Tona Pearce Myers

Library of Congress Cataloging-in-Publication Data
Makridakis, Marney K., date.
 Hop, skip, jump : 75 ways to playfully manifest a meaningful life / Marney K. Makridakis.
      pages   cm
Includes bibliographical references.
ISBN 978-1-60868-311-6 (paperback) — ISBN 978-1-60868-312-3 (ebook)
1. Play—Psychological aspects. 2. Creative ability. 3. Work-life balance.
I. Title.
BF717.M35 2014
158.1—dc23   2014022547

First printing, November 2014
ISBN 978-1-60868-311-6
Printed in the USA on 100% postconsumer-waste recycled paper

 New World Library is proud to be a Gold Certified Environmentally Responsible Publisher. Publisher certification awarded by Green Press Initiative. www.greenpressinitiative.org

10   9   8   7   6   5   4   3   2   1

FOR MY MOM
she plays with her books
creates and curates her games
her quiet brilliance

Contents

Section Two

Section Three   JUMP

Introduction

You have probably picked up this book because you want to *manifest* something — and it's likely something you see as being part of your meaningful life. You might want to manifest:

- A creative dream
- Improvements in physical health
- A soul mate
- A different job or profession
- Completion of an old, forgotten project
- A new home
- A meaningful community
- Transformation of an old belief or attitude
- A certain sum of money
- A fantasy vacation
- Change in the world

Of course, there are many more examples, but ultimately, *manifesting comes down to momentum*. Play invites you to connect to the power of momentum without even realizing it.

I believe in *a world where work feels like play*, and while it's not always as easy as I'd like, I try to spend as much time there as possible. My goal is to help you identify, activate, and use the *powerful intersections between play and productivity* in order to manifest whatever you desire. *Manifest* means to reveal what is already there, to take what already exists and make it clearly and plainly visible. My clients, many of whom are creative entrepreneurs, already have what they need to succeed — and likely so do you. However, I help my clients by introducing playful toys and tools that help them manifest their desires faster, and with more ease and joy.

Play can be applied to *anything*, even the most serious, unplayful topics. When writing this book, I reconnected with a friend I had not seen in over twenty years. She knew me in my tumultuous teens and early twenties, before I had been diagnosed with bipolar disorder and hit rock bottom. She asked me why I was writing books about creativity instead of books that help people recover from mental illness. Interestingly, her question made me realize that this book *is* about mental health recovery, only not just for those diagnosed with a disorder, but for *everyone* who wants to radically improve their day-to-day productivity or even make a Great Big Dream come true.

The playful processes I use today were things I was doing two decades ago to pick up the toppled ABC blocks of my life. Almost anything I've managed to make real in my life — emotional healing, creative business success, major health improvements, raising a child, concocting the ideal chai latte — has come from the spirit of play. So I continue to Hop, Skip, and Jump through this wild adventure of life, and in these pages, I invite you to join me as we explore all the sweet, surprising ways we can playfully manifest what we want in our lives. *Whatever* you want to manifest, you can use the ideas in this book to do so and create a life that matters to you while having fun doing it. This is your opportunity to remember how to laugh from your belly, try new things, and feel a bit silly as you play with who you are and how you move about your life. When you connect to the power of play, you tap into the spirit of adventure and experience the amazing feeling that everything is possible.

Why Play Matters

Ask anyone to define play, and they'll probably give an example rather than a definition. It's a tough thing to describe accurately.

It's fairly obvious to see the very general ways that play shows up in the human life cycle. Infants play to achieve emotional attunement and security. Preschoolers play to discover their sense of self and the world around them. Children play to develop imagination and social skills. Teenagers can play to explore their identity and express the spectrum of emotions. Twenty-somethings often play to escape real-world responsibilities and ever-increasing pressures of life. Adults of all ages use play as a reward that usually comes *after* working: choir practice in the evening, golf on the weekend, photography on a vacation, bird-watching and boating after retirement.

For adults, play can be much more than simply filling the open spaces between work and daily responsibilities. *Play is the portal to presence.* Play is the way you touch and amplify the enchantment of being human. Play is filled with contradictions — inspiring sophomoric pranks and high art, deconstruction and discovery, mindless escape and soulful expression. It is the thing that animals do without being taught and the state that humans crave without knowing exactly how to describe it.

When it comes to the intersection of play and productivity, the secret is quite simple: what moves us *is* what moves us, which simply means what moves us *emotionally* is what moves us to *action*. This is why play helps us be productive. Play is many, many things, but it is never still, stuck, or stagnant; it somehow always moves. So when it comes to manifesting a meaningful life, play *works*.

I have always been naturally inclined toward a playful approach to life, with an imagination broader than Disneyland. When I was about five years old, I was extremely frustrated because my little ponytailed head was filled with stories that I couldn't write down; I could sound out words but couldn't yet master the mechanical process of using a pencil. My dad had the crafty idea of introducing me to a typewriter to simplify the process, so that I could move more quickly, sounding out the words and pressing the letter keys. My early spelling included no vowels and no spaces between words, so those old stories look like some kind of strange encoded message from a vintage spy movie.

THE IMPACT OF PLAY

I am not a play theorist or researcher myself, nor do I play one on TV. But I find intellectual enjoyment in reading about the implications of play in fields such as science, history, and culture. This book includes a recommended reading list for those who, like me, enjoy reading about the influence of play on our lives. Here are some of my favorite facts about play, which, like the contestants in the Miss America pageants I watched as a child, are presented in no particular order:

- Rapid eye movement (REM) sleep and play share similar brainstem evolutionary patterns, which might account for the relaxing, restorative effects of play.
- In a study of homicidal young men in the 1960s, it was determined that "lack of play" was a key similarity among them, leading to theories about lack of play being connected to homicidal tendencies.
- Thanks to nineteenth-century scholars (Friedrich von Schiller, Herbert Spencer, Moritz Lazarus) and twentieth-century psychologists (Sigmund Freud, Karl Bühler, Jean Piaget), the psychological and cognitive sciences now include play theory.
- It has been proposed that play might provide a model of the variability that allows for "natural" selection and that evolution is, in fact, based on play.
- Play behaviors of both animals and children are extremely similar.
- The right to play is explicitly recognized in the Convention on the Rights of the Child, adopted by the General Assembly of the United Nations in 1989.
- Play is a major modality used in psychotherapy and behavior modification of children, building on Freud's assertion that watching children play is the best way to learn about them.
- Child life, a social work specialty introduced by Emma Plank in the 1960s and in widespread use in Western hospitals today,

employs play techniques to provide emotional support for pediatric patients and to aid them in the healing process.

- Studies of play in various countries have revealed details about the socialization practices, parenting beliefs, and traditions of the cultures being studied.
- When children's recess time at school is shortened, they perform more poorly on tests.
- The inclination to "play pretend" as a way to prepare for future roles is universal. This kind of play is observed worldwide, in both animals and humans, across cultures and demographics.
- One factor in the rise in obesity is the dramatic, sudden change in the kind of play presented to children, as more of the play landscape is related to video games and screen time.
- Even though there is more research on play theory than ever, studies show that the time children spend playing continues to decrease.
- No experiments have yet been done to test if play maintains "soulness" and "whaleness" (see below and page 6 for an explanation of this exciting new theory).

However, his plan worked; I wrote story after story, plunking away on that old typewriter. I had few childhood friends, but I created entire worlds of characters with whom I interacted regularly. The typewriter and page functioned as the playground for my imagination, and they still do today.

When I was diagnosed with and treated for bipolar disorder in my twenties, play is what helped me dig out from the unraveling tendrils of my mind. My natural inclinations toward color, whimsy, and unbridled fantasy are still, perhaps ironically, the very things that keep me sane and whole.

I'm looking at the last words of the sentence above, and I feel the uncontrollable urge to reverse the vowels so the word *sane* becomes *soul*, and *whole* becomes *whale*. Now I'm giggling because it feels like the ending of an intellectual poem:

> play keeps me
> soul and whale

Now I'm imagining myself teaching a class, reading these words and pretending they are a quotation from the library of philosophical poets. I can see the audience nodding their heads: "Play keeps me soul and whale....Ah yes. Amazingly put."

The previous paragraphs offer a close-up look at *my* play process, an example of how play keeps me going. Five minutes ago, I was writing along, talking about the importance of play. I confess I was feeling restless and craving pretzels. My mind was wandering to my manuscript deadline, and my inner critic was screaming, "This has all been said before."

But then...well, I decided to play a little bit, and now I'm smiling and feeling silly, and I've got lots of energy to keep writing. Plus, I'm quite confident that nobody has *ever* said "play keeps me soul and whale" before, so take *that*, you nasty inner critic. Here's the takeaway from your first lesson: at any time, *play is just two words away*.

TRY THIS: PLAY IS JUST TWO WORDS AWAY

1. Pick two words. *Any* two words. Really.
2. Complete this phrase using your two words: "Play keeps me _____ and _____."
3. Imagine this is a quote from a poem or someone famous. What in the world do you surmise it might mean?
4. Post your quote on the social media outlet of your choice, as if it were an actual quote. Watch the responses from your friends, and tag @ArtellaLand so I can see them, too. Trust me, *any* quote can be taken seriously, as long as it doesn't make sense.

There you go! Play Is Just Two Words Away is an easy, playful process to shift your mind-set in a matter of moments. You can try it whenever you notice you are "working hard," and it will quickly invite your neural pathways to a playful place. Your neurons will thank you.

This book shares seventy-five of my favorite playful processes that have worked well for me, my clients, and my imaginary friends, of which there are probably far more than I'd care to admit. Much inspiration also comes from my son, Kai, who has been my live-in expert on the subject of play for these first six years of his life and thus serves as our pint-size muse in these pages.

A Quick Romp through This Book

If you generally don't like to read a book cover to cover, you can relax. This is, above all, an *idea* book, here to help you access more play and productivity in your life, and to help you do it in your own way. You don't need to read this book in sequential order and should feel free to — you guessed it — hop, skip, and jump around the book.

You can use this book as a spontaneous companion, opening it whenever you want to add some playful fizz to your day. You can also use it as a creative guide for manifesting a specific project or goal, one spirited step at a time. If you are using the book to focus on a particular project, I suggest moving through the book in order, spending the most time with ideas and activities that tickle the playful parts of you.

Supplies

You will get the most from this book if you have some playful supplies handy as you read and romp. Here are some suggestions:

- Select a journal, diary, or notebook that will become a dedicated playbook for your Hop, Skip, Jump process.
- Gather colorful writing tools to use in your playbook, such as gel pens, colored pencils, bottles of glitter glue, lipstick, colored markers, tubes of cake frosting, and — especially — crayons. Crayons have a built-in ability to activate a childlike mind-set, and I highly recommend using them throughout this process. It might feel a little

weird at first — it isn't easy to write legibly with crayons. But the simple act of using a crayon is so effective when it comes to tapping into a playful spirit that I strongly encourage you to at least give it a try.

- Consciously gather more toys around you in your day-to-day life. You can find retired toys in thrift stores, at garage sales, and often in your own drawers and closets; they are eager for a second career and would love to serve you. Place more toys and playthings where you can see them, touch them, and yes, *play* with them! You can become more aware of the presence of play by having playthings around you.

Fun, Frolicsome Features

As you move through each chapter, you'll encounter lots of things along the way to keep the experience fun and playful, such as:

- *Fun Facts* — trivia and tidbits about toys and playthings that begin each chapter. The Fun Facts are followed by questions to help you reflect on your own play process.
- *Top Ten Lists* — humorous lists sprinkled throughout the book that function as a prescription for healthy levity. Take two chuckles and call me in the morning.
- *Haikoodles* — haiku about play, just waiting to be drawn and doodled by you! As you read each short poem, take a play break and draw or doodle in the book's margins or in your notebook or journal.
- *AcroWhims and Manifestagrams* — revolutionarily ridiculous riffs at the end of each chapter, defined as follows:

  AcroWhim *n.*, a whimsical acronym in which an existing word functions as a magical abbreviation for an important message — for example: PLAY = Purposeful Love, Activating Yes.

  Manifestagram *n.*, an anagram with manifesting powers, having letters that can be rearranged to playfully reveal an important message — for example: Manifest = "Amen" fits!

Why include all these fun tangents? Simple: if you're smiling, you won't pay attention to how many pages you've read or how much you're learning. That is what momentum is all about. *Momentum* comes from *moments*, those amazing moments when you are so engaged you don't even realize you are being productive.

Play and productivity are no longer two separate worlds that rarely meet. They can come together like happy fistfuls of Play-Doh, beautifully blending to reveal the brand-new colors of a meaningful life. You get to play *and* do. Play matters. Your life matters. It's time to manifest.

A QUIRKY QUIZ: DISCOVERING YOUR MANIFESTING MOVES

In this book, I use the words *Hop*, *Skip*, and *Jump* to refer to three phases of the manifestation process. Later in the introduction, I explain these three phases in detail, but first, here is a quirky quiz that invites you to take a look at your natural inclinations when manifesting. (You can take it online at www.artellaland.com/hsj -quiz.html.)

For the most helpful results to this quiz, choose answers that most accurately reflect your *natural* mode, your core instincts, rather than things you might be "working on" or trying to change. In other words, answer from who you *really* are rather than who you wish you could be or who you might be with just a little effort. To distinguish this nuance, it might be helpful to use language such as "I would love to be *x*, but when it comes down to it, I'm really *y*." Also keep in mind that there is absolutely nothing hierarchical about the three phases; one is not better than another.

This is some serious play, so grab your crayons and notebook, and let's begin:

1. This phrase is most true about me:
   a. I love to dream.
   b. I love to dabble.
   c. I love to *do*.

2. I am generally most comfortable and relaxed when I am:
   a. planning.
   b. puttering.
   c. producing.

3. I feel most like myself when I am:
   a. musing and dreaming in a relaxed state of wonder and curiosity.
   b. meandering through possibilities and trying new things.
   c. moving something to completion as quickly as possible.

4. When they need support, my closest friends are most likely to come to me for:
   a. listening, holding space, compassion, and empathy.
   b. back-and-forth discussion to share new perspectives and a variety of possibilities.
   c. quick solutions, practical advice, and an action plan.

5. My true nature is most comfortable:
   a. exploring.
   b. experimenting.
   c. executing.

6. When giving a birthday gift, I'm most looking forward to:
   a. thinking about what the recipient would like, dreaming, brainstorming, and making mental notes of my ideas.
   b. window-shopping at various locations or sources, taking my time to look at different things.
   c. the moment when I get to give the gift and experience the recipient's reaction.

7. When acting naturally, I am most likely to:
   a. do a lot of dreaming, research, and preparation before taking action.
   b. do a lot of play and experimentation before taking action.
   c. quickly take action without doing a lot of planning or experimenting first.

8. If I were locked in a room for an entire day to do nothing but fully explore my vision for the coming five years, I would most likely:
   a. be in heaven!
   b. enjoy the process but probably feel overwhelmed by all the new ideas flowing in.
   c. be fighting the feeling that I wasn't being very productive.
9. A personal journal or notebook of mine would most likely consist primarily of:
   a. musings, thoughts, lists, and ideas about one or two particular topics.
   b. ideas running the gamut of topics and themes, with new topics coming up all the time.
   c. step-by-step action plans for things happening in the next week.
10. The kind of frustration I experience most often is:
    a. when I have an idea, I have a hard time knowing how to get started.
    b. I begin lots of things but feel like I never get anywhere.
    c. I am great at follow-through, but the results don't match my expectations.
11. When I get a new idea, I'm most likely to get stuck:
    a. when the idea leaves the theoretical or conceptual stage and I'm not sure what to do.
    b. when the idea inevitably expands into more and more ideas and takes me in so many directions that I lose focus on what I really want.
    c. when I've brought the idea to life but realize I've skipped some important steps along the way.
12. I am most likely to regret:
    a. not taking action.
    b. getting sidetracked or distracted.
    c. jumping in before thinking things through.

13. The people who know me well admire me for:
    a. solid vision, thorough planning, and self-awareness.
    b. my varied pursuits and interesting life experiences.
    c. how much I seem to get done.
14. I'd be most likely criticized for:
    a. conceptualizing an idea for a long time, without taking much action.
    b. having too many ideas, distractions, and in-progress projects, and not being focused.
    c. being too impulsive, unrealistic, or acting based on all-or-nothing thinking.
15. When I think of "manifesting a meaningful life," I know I'm good at:
    a. tapping into what it *feels* like — if only I knew what it would entail!
    b. holding many, many possibilities that would make me happy — if only I could follow through and focus!
    c. acting very quickly to do whatever I set my mind to — if only I could get the results I want!
16. If I were told to "take action," my response would be:
    a. "How do I even start?"
    b. "How do I pick which project?"
    c. "Okay! Here are the next three things I will do."

Scoring Your Quiz

To score the quiz, count the number of *a*, *b*, and *c* answers. If you have eight or more of any one letter, it indicates you have a natural comfort for one of the three phases:

If you have eight or more *a*'s, you are most comfortable in the Hop phase. *Your manifestation strength is the organic ability to connect to your vision and plans, to get your dreams on solid ground.* You are skilled at making preparations, although sometimes those preparations might just exist in your head. This book will help you continue to have fun in your comfortable Hop phase but also break out of your comfort zone to try more new things, gain momentum, and take action to turn those visions into realities.

If you have eight or more *b*'s, you are most at home in the Skip phase. *Your manifestation strength is the variety of things that excite you, your willingness to try them, and your natural skill at creating momentum.* You are a lively person with a rich connection to the world around you. You may feel judged by yourself or others for "skipping around too much," but this book will help you understand and accept this as your core strength, and have fun building on it! You will also learn how bolstering your natural craving for variety with grounded visions and tangible action steps will make your manifesting experiences more satisfying and exciting.

If you have eight or more *c*'s, you are most naturally aligned with the Jump phase. *Your manifestation strength is taking action, sustaining momentum, and moving things to completion.* You may get criticized for not thinking things through or not looking before you leap. You may regret moving too quickly or missing some steps along the way. This book will help you learn how to increase the effectiveness of your natural inclination to "ready, fire, aim" by balancing it with stronger foundations that will increase the success and sustainability of the things you create.

If you don't have at least eight answers in any one letter, *you have manifestation strengths in several areas* — your core inclinations are spread between two stages, or perhaps evenly distributed across all three. You likely have had successful experiences with manifesting things you want in your life, but you might find yourself wondering why everything feels like so much work and wishing you were more satisfied and content with your life. If your answers are spread across multiple categories, this book will put your natural inner harmony to even greater use, as you become more playful and productive in creating the life of your dreams.

Your Own Customized Manifestation Process

Hop, Skip, and Jump represent three distinct energies that can work together harmoniously. This book is about playfully activating the energies of *all three* phases so that your manifestation process becomes a lot more robust and, especially, a lot more fun. You do not have to be something you are not or move out of your natural lane. Rather, I'm inviting you to try some new possibilities, let yourself learn how to recover your child's heart and mind, smile in spite of yourself, and have so much fun you won't even realize you're making great progress, faster than before.

More and more people are seeing that creativity and productivity go hand in hand. This book introduces the values of a right-brained approach to productivity, such as those shown in the table below.

Left-Brain Approach	Right-Brain Approach
Believe it when you see it	Believe it, then see it
Celebrating when complete	Celebrating before beginning
Based on priorities — what is most important	Based on *glorities* — what is most glorious
Separating the big and little view	Holding the macro and micro views simultaneously
Step-by-step, linear action	Spiraling, nonlinear movement
Fueled by results	Motivated by momentum
Independence based	Support enriched
Breakthroughs from external acts	Breakthroughs from internal shifts
Hard work	Deep play

In the right-brained approach, *all three phases are equally important.* As we create meaningful lives, we often stumble when we miss crucial parts of the manifestation process — in other words, when we don't spend enough time or energy in a particular phase. For example, I am most comfortable in the Jump phase, so my natural inclination is to spend very little time in the Hop and Skip stages. However, I make the most progress when I accentuate the aspects of me that are naturally strong *and* gently activate those other aspects of the process that may not come naturally. Play is an amazingly effective way to activate the manifestation skills that are not part of your natural repertoire, to help you create more successful, sustainable results.

Hop, Skip, Jump:
Three Playful Manifestation Phases

The common expression "a hop, skip, and a jump" implies ease and a short distance. We often use it when referring to something in physical proximity or a minimal quantitative time away — for example, "We're a hop, skip, and a jump away from the store." However, in this book, *Hop, Skip,* and *Jump* refer to qualitative experiences rather than quantitative ones. I wrote my first book, *Creating Time,* to share the idea that our lives are actually ruled by *qualitative,* rather than quantitative, time. We don't measure our lives by how long something takes. In the end, what matters most is how much meaning we have experienced in the process. Our *experiences* of meaning are what manifest a meaningful life.

Successful manifestation unfolds through the three phases of Hop, Skip, and Jump. However, the quality of time, energy, and pleasure experienced in each phase varies greatly, based on our natural tendencies and conscious choices. I summarize these phases as follows:

- *Hopping* refers to having an idea or impulse and exploring it in your imagination.
- *Skipping* refers to experimenting and trying new things.
- *Jumping* refers to quickly moving into action.

Think of *anything* you've manifested in your life, and if you look closely, I believe you'll see that you touched on each of these phases in some way, though likely spending more time in some phases than others. If you look at the things you want but have *not* yet manifested, you will likely realize you have not hit all three phases yet, or perhaps have not explored them all fully.

The Language of the Body

It is interesting to look at the physical movements associated with each of the three phases. Chris Hammer, a physical therapist and Rubenfeld Synergist, discussed the physical attributes of each with me. According to Chris, "All three skills prepare us to safely and efficiently navigate all the many different environments we must meet in our day. For children, these movements are an integral part of play, which is their learning ground."

Here are the different ways each phase contributes to physical development:

In hopping, muscles are strengthened and balance is developed, as the body stays in one place. Hopping on one foot is a key gross motor skill for children that prepares the way for more complex skills. As Chris pointed out to me, "When hopping, we need to switch feet in order to avoid tiring. It is not something that can be sustainable for a long time." *The goal of hopping is to gain coordination, balance, and the necessary stability to negotiate all the varied terrain we walk on.*

In skipping, the body moves multidirectionally. The movement is spontaneous, varying in speed as alternating feet act as the accelerator. "Skipping requires coordination to quickly alternate feet as well as adding a little hop before switching feet," Chris explained. "The rest of the body organizes to assist in this fast movement." Of the three movements, skipping covers the most area. *The goal of skipping is to cover the most ground as easily and quickly as possible.*

In jumping from one place to another, the body moves out and forward. Chris described jumping as "the relationship between propulsion and power, as we accelerate our body mass to get off the ground with both legs." Jumping from one place to another is distinguished by its conscious execution and by the fact that it has clear launch and destination points. *The goal of jumping is to gather power and energy to move from one place to another with a single, clear movement.*

The following table lists the goals, advantages, and potential risks of each phase. Happily, you can experience the advantages whenever the phase is activated, even if it is activated just a little bit. You can also easily counterbalance the potential risks by stimulating the other phases.

Phase	Goals	Advantages	Potential Risks
Hop	To take your time dreaming, musing, planning, and envisioning. To enjoy your dream without pressure to perform. To save time later by being here now.	Ideas are gathered and clarified. Embodying the vision feels good without having to wait for a payoff. Planning and envisioning save time later. Becoming balanced and grounded provides a strong foundation and commitment.	Momentum can be lost when the next steps are not known. You can have difficulty identifying resources, support, and action steps when ideas stay in conceptual or theoretical form. The initial enthusiasm can wane quickly due to overthinking.
Skip	To be at peace with experimenting and trying new things. To embrace process rather than product. To trust your instincts to tell you where to go next. To fully enjoy and appreciate a variety of things in order to gain momentum.	Trying lots of different things yields valuable information. Spontaneity brings a feeling of freedom. Becoming aware of what you like and don't like provides clarity. Consistent, enjoyable experimentation creates momentum.	You can experience doubt, disorganization, and a feeling of being overwhelmed, with few results to show for it. Self-judgments and judgments of others may get in the way. Being stuck between dreaming and doing can feel confusing when there isn't a clear intention to complete something.

continued on next page

Phase	Goals	Advantages	Potential Risks
Jump	To take action and make things happen. To make a choice and follow through. To bring ideas to completion and full manifestation.	Fast-paced action brings an adrenaline rush. Completion and execution feel rewarding. Receiving a response from others provides additional feedback. A habit of completion makes it easier to sustain action.	Becoming too focused on results can cloud the process. Projects and ideas may not be planned or tested adequately. Extreme disappointment can arise if all energy has been channeled but results don't match expectations.

Sample Scenarios

You don't have to change who you are in order to succeed. You can, however, have a lot more fun when you use play to experiment with some approaches that you've never tried before. The Hop, Skip, and Jump phases work together; your core strengths will always serve you well, but they are especially powerful when you combine your natural approach with the other phases.

Consider the following scenarios, and notice how each person could benefit from staying true to his or her natural approach while also activating other phases:

LAURA has spent a long time with the same dream: to open a family-friendly yoga studio. She has envisioned it fully, and is completely committed to the way her idea will look and how it will serve her community. She has taken a few actions, usually with a lot of time in between them, during which her momentum fell flat. She is very strong in the Hop phase. It would really help if she could activate the Skip phase so she could follow her own energy and take more frequent small steps, build joy, and gain momentum. With a bit more momentum through Skipping, her strong purpose and vision will naturally lead her to action and completion.

JIM has dozens of interests and many skills. He gets lots of ideas and usually takes a step or two, then gets distracted when he sees something else that captures his interest. He longs to make some kind of meaningful contribution to the world; but he has labeled himself a "chronic dabbler" and shoots himself down whenever he gets a new idea. For example, he had an idea to start a specialized radio show and fully enjoyed a few days of tinkering with the idea. Then he learned about pinwheel photography, went out and bought supplies, and signed up for a local class. As the months went by, whenever he thought of the radio show, he felt embarrassed that he never did anything with it, though he's started lots of other things since then. His core strength is in the Skip phase. By activating the Jump phase, he could get to know and understand completion energy in his own way, and gain the much-needed self-confidence to take important steps toward his goals.

MARIE is used to acting very quickly; she gets an idea and acts fast. Her idea to knit hats for children was no different. She made a couple of prototypes, took them to a local store, got an order, and launched into production. However, she quickly tired of knitting the same model over and over, and wished she would have thought things through before committing. She also felt frustrated when she learned that customers liked her hats but they were too big for most children. She is very strong in the Jump phase, but with *all* of her energy in that aspect of the manifestation process, she becomes quite disheartened when the results aren't thrilling. She would benefit from exploring the Hop phase and learning how she can feel satisfied by things other than the emotional rush she gets from quick completion. By strengthening the other phases, her grounded commitment and conscious planning will help her make the necessary adjustments when things don't go as planned.

Do you see yourself in any of these examples?

Now *you* get to explore the energies of Hop, Skip, and Jump — through the use of play. There are twenty-five ideas for each phase, so you'll find lots to try! They are presented in a loose order for those following this book as a sequential manifestation guide, but you can pick any of them as a stand-alone method for holding your Hop, stimulating your Skip, or jazzing up your Jump!

SECTION ONE

1

From Plato to Play-To

FUN FACT: In 2006, a Play-Doh fragrance was created in celebration of Play-Doh's fiftieth anniversary. According to Hasbro, the special fragrance was "meant for highly creative people, who seek a whimsical scent reminiscent of their childhood."

What scents remind you of playful moments in your childhood?
How might you reconnect with those scents in your life today?

lato quoted Socrates as saying, "The unexamined life is not worth living." These famous words may have unintentionally kick-started the entire self-help industry. While we are so fortunate to live in a time when we have seemingly infinite resources to support us in examining our lives, one might argue that our culture has become rather *over*examined. Existing merely with the goal of self-examination can keep you stuck in a place of exploring inwardly rather than expressing outwardly. It's also an easy way to get really, really bored with yourself.

A Foundational Philosophy of Play

One way to define a meaningful life at its fullest is *expression in action.* It happens when you take something from inside and create it on the outside. This is true even if nobody else sees what you manifest. If you want to have better dental hygiene, it's not enough to just get the idea. You need to adjust any beliefs that stand in the way; you need to try a few different ways to do it; and you need to start using the right brush, floss, or Waterpik and stay motivated to keep using them. It doesn't matter if anyone else ever notices (though I imagine your dentist and your significant other would) — you have taken an idea from the inside and expressed it on the outside.

To approach manifestation playfully, your first step is to create a foundational philosophy of play. We can use Plato to inspire us. We could also use Play-Doh, but that might be a little messier. Besides, you might not have any Play-Doh handy, or at least not nearly enough multicolored canisters to adequately express yourself, because you just started this book and haven't fully embraced your playful side yet. Just wait — you will!

Your playful journey starts with *the words you say* about what you want. A play-to philosophy can be constructed simply by inserting "play to" in any statement about your goal. The table below gives some examples.

Statement about Your Goal	Reformulated as a Play-To Statement
I want to lose weight.	I will play to lose weight.
I want to increase my prosperity.	I will play to increase my prosperity.
I want to spend more time with my family.	I will play to spend more time with my family.
I want to manage my time better.	I will play to manage my time better.

TRY THIS: CREATE YOUR PLAY-TO PHILOSOPHY

To create a meaningful life, the first step is to define *meaning*. What does *meaning* mean to you? Connect with *your* meaning of *meaning* and not some meanie's meaning of *meaning*. (Can you imagine the field day my editor is having with this playful stuff?) The bottom line is that *meaning is personal to you*, and you get to create it yourself.

1. Grab your crayons and draw a big circle on a piece of paper. In the center, write, "My Meaningful Life." Feel free to sing "Circle of Life" from *The Lion King* as you draw. Or not.

2. Fill the page with words, phrases, and doodles that represent a meaningful life. Fill the entire page. Turn it upside down. Write big and write small. Try different colors of markers or crayons, as colors help activate play. Write words in different languages, preferably made-up ones.

3. After your word collage is complete, write a list of goals that will help you move closer to what is inside your circle of meaning. Write them in the format "I want to..."

4. Finally, rewrite each goal or intention as a play-to statement. As a reminder of the extremely fancy technique shared above, this means taking a phrase like "I want to get a new job" and substituting the words "play to" so that it becomes "I will play to get a new job." This is your play-to philosophy. *It all starts with your words.* This stuff works. Or better said, "plays."

ACROWHIM
PLAY-TO = Passionate Living Allows You To Open

HAIKOODLE

play as colored clay
little balls rolled in your hands
ellipses to fun

TIME TO DOODLE

TOP TEN SIGNS
YOU HAVEN'T FIGURED OUT YOUR TRUE PASSION

10. You're a preferred member of the Career-a-Month Book Club.
9. Instead of a business card, you have a business *deck*.
8. You're so fearful of having to make an "elevator speech" about your work that you always take the stairs.
7. You now consider lunchtime to be a peak experience.
6. Your relationship with your snooze button is more intimate than your relationship with your partner.
5. You launch into an explanation of your directionless woes when a telemarketer asks you how you're doing.
4. You sign your letters, "Sincerely, I think."
3. Every third book on your shelf has the word *lost* in it.
2. You tell yourself, "On the upside, if every day is a midlife crisis, doesn't that mean I'll live forever?"
1. You burst into tears whenever a child says, "I know what I want to be when I grow up."

2 Playfully Pressing the Reset Button

FUN FACT: Lego's name comes from the Danish phrase *log godt*, which means "play well."

Think of Lego as also meaning "let go."
How might "playing well" and "letting go" be connected?

One of the components of the Hop phase is creating new beliefs that support everything you think, feel, and do. Your beliefs are like a computer's operating system. If you stay working within an old operating system, you can't produce what you want without a lot of errors. The awakening comes when you realize that your belief system can be upgraded whenever you like. If the metaphor of your belief system as an operating system feels too much like work, let's try something else: you can look to the windows of your soul instead of Windows on your computer or pay attention to the fruits of your imagination instead of the Macintosh on your desk. When it comes to representing operating systems, this is an equal opportunity book.

Creating New Beliefs

We live in a time when inspiration and information are everywhere. The influx of information coming at us blends in a big soup with our personal stories and history, until somehow we can't even taste our own beliefs anymore. This is even harder when book titles are literally insulting us, calling us "dummies" or "idiots."

Whenever you read a book — be it one with an insulting title or not — and find yourself confused, overwhelmed, or befuddled, you lose a piece of yourself. If you were given a book about manifesting that was written in Mandarin Chinese and you did not speak Mandarin, you would simply say, "Oh, this isn't in my language. This book isn't for me." You would not shrink into self-doubt and despair, and think that something is wrong with you. You would simply keep looking to find a book that lines up with who you are. This is an example of a new belief: *I don't need to change who I am, and I believe I can find whatever I need.*

While there is much written about *how* to get things done, there is little revealed about the energetics *behind and beneath* getting things done, which are braided within your beliefs. What's happening underneath the action or inaction in your life? What arc you believing, or not believing, that influences your experiences of success? Aligning with new beliefs doesn't need to be a heavy, soul-wrenching experience. Here's a fun way to give your belief system a fresh start:

TRY THIS: MAKE YOUR RESET BUTTON

1. Right now, take a piece of paper and draw a great big rectangle on it. In the middle, write the word "RESET" in large letters. This is the reset button for your belief system, and you can press it anytime you like.
2. Press the button. Which finger did you use? Try another one, just for fun, 'cause that is what this is all about.
3. Press the button with fingers on your nondominant hand. Then press it with your palm, your elbow, your chin. Eventually, you'll probably either be cracking up or thinking I'm cracked up. Both are correct.

Yes, it might seem a little silly to press a simple doodle with different parts of your body. However, if you can allow yourself to truly *feel* the experience, and have fun with it, you will notice a profound change as your body realizes that you are not stuck in an old iteration of yourself and that your beliefs are not fixed in time.

MANIFESTAGRAM
Press the reset button = He stops: Trust. Enter. Be.

HAIKOODLE

play as a button
connecting the vest of life
holds dreams together

3 Your Celebration Manifesto

*If you were gathering a band together to sing
your own celebration song, who would be in the band,
and what would your group be called?*

When I suggest that someone celebrate *before* a project is begun, I am often met with a doubtful response — something like one of these:

"That doesn't sound very productive."

"My friends and family would think I was crazy."

"Right now, all I can see is a big project in front of me. I frankly don't feel like celebrating."

Manifestos Help You Celebrate

Resistance to celebrating at the beginning of a project is a sign that you need to create a new belief: *initiation energy and completion energy are equally valuable.* The Hop phase is just as important as the Jump phase, though we don't get a lot of affirmation of that out there in the serious world. This is why manifestos are important, and Karl Marx was trending before trending was trendy.

When completing an exercise about goals, Amy declared that she wanted to be "gracious, spacious, playcious." Now *that's* a manifesto! It also sounds like the name of a band. I will find out if she is available to be booked at your celebration, and get back to you.

Writing a celebration manifesto is a party you can have all by yourself. Your new, positive beliefs are the guests, and the old, limiting beliefs are not invited. If you are rolling your eyes right now, then you are experiencing a very odd physiological phenomenon that you should really get checked out, what with being able to read *while* your eyes are rolling. For those who have returned to reading after eye rolling: welcome back. You *can* do this, no matter how you are feeling right now. When Sandra was totally overwhelmed, I invited her to stay right where she was — tired, sad, frustrated — and create a celebration manifesto right then and there, using the prompts below. It instantly changed her energy and helped her find her playful self again.

TRY THIS: MANIFEST, OH!

1. Complete the following prompts in writing. Keep the phrases as they are, because repetition of the same word creates momentum as you write.

    I am here today to celebrate _____.
    I laugh out loud, and I celebrate _____.
    I cry a little, and I celebrate _____.
    I look to my questions, and I celebrate _____.
    I look to trusting what feels impossible, and I celebrate

    _____.

    I look to my choices, and I celebrate _____.
    I look to my new beliefs, and I celebrate _____.

2. You have just completed your celebration manifesto! Take a moment to read it out loud to yourself.

3. Now go to a mirror, and sing "Celebration" by Kool and the Gang if you know it, in which case dancing is optional, though probably inevitable. Now, as you make eye contact with yourself in the mirror, read your celebration manifesto. Let doubt, anxiety, and worry melt away…into play!

> ### ACROWHIM
> CELEBRATE = Call Everyone…
> Let Emotion Bring Radiant And Tantalizing Energy!

HAIKOODLE
play as a party
confetti evidence helps
picking up pieces

4 Parties and Presence

FUN FACT: The yo-yo is believed to be the second-oldest toy in the world, after dolls. The word *yo-yo* comes from a Filipino expression meaning "come-come."

What new energy in your life is ready to "come-come"?

Some people live their lives on the string of a yo-yo; they go up and down, waiting to finally be happy with themselves, without ever stopping long enough to know what fulfillment even means.

The Businessman and the Fisherman

The classic tale of the businessman and the fisherman beautifully captures how a switch in perspective can open the possibilities for so many gifts to come-come into your life:

> A wealthy businessman who was on vacation befriended a village fisherman. The fisherman lived simply, and while the two men couldn't be more different, they struck up a friendship. The wealthy man couldn't resist sharing business advice with the fisherman. He told the fisherman how he could expand his profits and eventually buy

another boat, and then another, and thus exponentially increase his revenue, following a traditional Western return-on-investment paradigm.

The fisherman said, "That sounds like a lot of work. Why would I want to do that?" Without missing a beat, the businessman extolled all the amazing benefits of a successful life: "It is exactly what I did! I focused on building my business, expanding my reach, decreasing my costs, increasing my profits. Eventually, I will be able to retire, live in a beautiful and remote place, be on the water all day and relax as I fish, and spend time with my family. That is the kind of freedom I will have, and all my hard work will be worth it!"

The fisherman smiled and said, "My friend, this is what I *already* do. I spend all day on the water and relax as I fish. I go home and spend time with my family. I am completely free right now. I don't have to wait to retire."

This is a wonderful story and one that I often repeat inside my mind, not unlike *One Fish, Two Fish, Red Fish, Blue Fish* by Dr. Seuss in the days when Kai was demanding that I read it at least twelve and a half times daily.

What would happen if Dr. Seuss told the classic tale above? See the sidebar for the answer. Whenever you get caught up in the old story "I have to work hard so I'll be able to play," you can keep this story in mind.

Don't Wait to Retire

What if you looked for opportunities to embrace play right now, instead of waiting for the work to be finished first? Lisa wanted to write a book, and as part of our work together, we designed an action map for her. When I asked her which of the steps felt like something she really wanted to do, her first response was an honest one: she didn't want to do any of it; it all looked overwhelming. I asked her to look again. She admitted that the very last step — to have a book launch party — seemed fun. I suggested that

THE STORY OF THE BUSINESSMAN AND THE FISHERMAN IN THE STYLE OF DR. SEUSS

Businessman says:

> One fish, two fish
> I see you fish
> You don't have a clue, fish
> You must accrue fish
> When you're in *Who's Who*, fish
> *Then* you can be through, fish

Fisherman replies:

> I must say, in lieu, fish
> Of what you say is true, fish
> I already *do* fish
> So I'll say "no thank *you*," fish

she plan her book launch party right now. It took a bit of convincing, but she did it. She had fun dreaming up invitations, decorations, and activities that might be involved. She had so much fun planning this party, she didn't even realize that she was actually creating content for her book; in fact, she created enough content to put together her book proposal. Her momentum was sky high, so the steps that once seemed overwhelming were now doable and even fun.

Why wait until you retire to do something you love? Why wait until something is *done* to catch a fish or throw a party? A big ole party can really give your belief system a boost. With sprinkles on top.

TRY THIS: MAKE YOUR PARTY INVITATIONS

Imagine that you're going to throw an amazing birthday party for your new project and you're designing invitations. This is a great ritual whenever you get a new idea or want to add some zest to something that's been somersaulting around in your mind. Ask yourself:

- What is the message on the invitation?
- Is there a theme for the gathering?
- Who is on the guest list?
- What would make this party even more special?

MANIFESTAGRAM
Birthday party = Bid thy art. Pray.

HAIKOODLE
play as a small child
learns how to hop on one foot
percussive success

5 Hopping with Hope

FUN FACT: It takes eighty feet of wire to make a Slinky, which collapses to only a few inches high.

Imagine your hope is like a Slinky. What makes your hope collapse to its minimum size? What makes your hope stretch out and expand? In which state do you spend the most time?

Whenever I hear the phrase "a spring in your step," a childhood memory of playing with a Slinky on a stairway comes to mind. With just the right positioning, the Slinky could "walk" down the stairs and even gain momentum while doing so. The 1970s TV commercials made it look easy, but in reality, it was a bit tricky; you had to get the starting position just right, not too close and not too far from the edge of the step. As a rather impetuous and impatient child, I would often give up and move on when something didn't work, but there was an intrigue about the Slinky that kept me trying and trying, hoping and hoping.

The Meaning of Hope

Hope is crucial during the Hop phase of manifesting. Without hope, you don't have the fuel you need to keep Hopping. Some linguists suggest an etymological connection between *hope*, from the Old English *hopian* ("to expect"), and *hop*, based on the idea of a "leap in expectation." Simplistic linguistic sophistics aside, Hop and hope are definitely related. When you fully take your time to embody the Hop phase, you get to fully experience hope.

Hope is the springy, squishy connection between you and making your dream happen. Like the Slinky, hope expands and contracts; you are the one who is stretching it, moving it between your hands, or even hopping with it down the stairs, like in the old TV commercials.

TRY THIS: MAKE A HOPE ROPE

Here are steps to make a physical representation of what holds you and your dream together: a hope rope.

1. Write down all the things you love about your dream on small slips of paper.
2. Tape the slips together in a paper chain. This is your hope rope!
3. You can continually add more links to the chain, to extend the hope rope whenever you like, adding more and more things that you love about your dream.
4. Whenever you are feeling low, you can take a moment to reflect on your hope rope and be reminded of your hope.

SMALL PRINT: The hope rope is not fit for dragging, pulling, or hauling heavy objects, nor for climbing on to perform circus tricks. The hope rope is, however, able to carry up to two tons of belief while swinging through infinite amounts of joy.

ACROWHIM
HOPE = Healing Opens, Possibility Enters

HAIKOODLE

play as a long rope
tethering togetherness
you can turn; I'll jump

6 Got Confidence?

FUN FACT: In 1954, a member of President Eisenhower's staff named Thomas Edwin Stevens gave paint-by-number kits to cabinet secretaries and White House visitors, and then framed and displayed their paintings in the West Wing corridor.

If you were to put your dream up on the wall,
what kind of frame would you use? Can you describe it?

We tend to think of confidence as being an *external* quality. We think of things like speaking with confidence, walking with confidence, writing with confidence, ordering an intricate latte with confidence. Even our terminology — "to get confidence" — has an implication that confidence is somehow outside of us. The "Got Milk?" campaign works because we see Heidi Klum's white mustache and know that yeah, she's got milk, or at least a good Photoshop artist. But what would a "Got Confidence?" campaign look like? How do you know when you have it?

Allowing Confidence

For starters, forget about *getting* confidence, and try just playing with it and allowing it in. The act of *allowing confidence* is just as important as making the phone call or joining the gym or sending out the book proposal or any external action you can take.

Confidence is an "inside job," a phrase that immediately brings wall-to-wall carpeting to mind. You might say that confidence is a plush rug for your soul.

In the Hop phase, confidence can sometimes be fleeting. You'll have moments when you feel full of belief and self-assuredness, and then inspiration amnesia sinks in. Here's a playful tool to help you remember:

TRY THIS: SIGNS OF CONFIDENCE

As your confidence grows inside, it still helps to have some outside reassurance. Imagine that every time you felt a twinge of doubt, you could see signs that you are on the right path. You can! You just have to make them.

1. Take a large piece of paper and write on it, "I can DO this!" This will literally be your sign of confidence.
2. Decorate and embellish it. As you create your sign, feel new levels of confidence taking residence in your body. Reflect on your readiness to express your gifts in the world. Allow these feelings to become part of the artwork itself.
3. Put the sign up on your wall.
4. Repeat for as many signs as you like. Studies show that more signs lead to more confidence. (Actually, I have no idea if studies have been done, but I invite you to initiate one, as conducting a study is a very Hoppy thing to do.)

MANIFESTAGRAM
Your confidence = Yo, nice fun credo!

HAIKOODLE

play as a big sign
"For rent or sale, sign up now!"
no reservations

7 Twenty-Eight Magic Minutes

FUN FACT: A typical child spends twenty-eight minutes a day coloring.

If you could do anything for twenty-eight minutes right now, purely for the sake of enjoyment, what would you do?

Let's play a game: Imagine that any twenty-eight-minute segment of your day could serve as a guaranteed predictor for the rest of that day. Each day holds a twenty-eight-minute pocket with a magnetic secret inside its ticking seconds — whatever you are doing and feeling during those twenty-eight minutes is *exactly* how you will feel for the rest of the day. What would you choose to do for your twenty-eight magic minutes to set the tone for the rest of the day?

The Hidden Magic Minutes

What would your life be like if these twenty-eight magic minutes were understood and implicit in your life but you didn't know *which* twenty-eight-minute segment held the magic? I imagine you might pay a lot more attention to what's happening during the day! If you caught yourself in a bad mood or thinking negatively, you would very quickly learn the habit of stopping yourself, realizing — uh-oh! — you might be in the twenty-eight magic minutes and so it would benefit you to change your tune.

Identifying how you'd use your twenty-eight magic minutes is a useful exercise. It helps you get in touch with who you are and how you Hop in the world.

TRY THIS: MANIFESTING MINUTES

Try these journaling prompts to explore your twenty-eight magic minutes. If possible, use crayons, colored pencils, or markers. Remember to have fun — after all, these could be your twenty-eight magic minutes right now!

1. If I could do something every day for twenty-eight minutes that would ensure that I'd feel great the rest of the day, I would _____.
2. If I never knew which twenty-eight minutes were the magic ones, I would _____.
3. The biggest way this would change my life would be _____.
4. If I lived that way right now, it might mean _____.
5. If something I'm dreading or putting off were actually part of the twenty-eight minutes, I might try _____.

ACROWHIM
MINUTES = Maybe I Need to
Understand Time Equality Soon

HAIKOODLE

play as a minute
building block of every day
time flies; so do I

FUN FACT: The "alphabet song" is sung to the same tune in countries all over the world, with different alphabet letters. The melody is believed to have been first written down by a French composer in 1761, and many composers — including Mozart and Haydn — have provided variations.

Describe the life you want to manifest,
to the tune of the alphabet song
(it doesn't have to rhyme or make sense).

Many children learn the alphabet, the very foundation of learning to read and write, by singing the alphabet song. The alphabet song is a great example of work that feels like play; kids are *learning* without realizing it. Alphabet books, blocks, puzzles, and games offer the same opportunity for children to be exposed to educational concepts through the natural act of playing.

The New ABCs: Actions, Beliefs, and Choices

When it comes to the manifesting process, *ABCs* stands for "actions, beliefs, and choices." When we think about moving a goal forward, we naturally think of *action*, and yet action is only part of the picture. The other two pieces are your *beliefs* and your *choices*. When the three components are not in alignment, you will stay stuck. When they are working together, you experience ease, flow, and forward movement.

The traditional way of looking at goals — that breakthroughs are the result of a big external effort — no longer has a place in today's overstimulated age because our adrenal systems are already operating on overdrive. The new way is to realize, finally, that breakthroughs happen not when action itself is the goal, but *when action is the result of internal alignment*. Robert Henri said about painting, "The object is not to make art, but to be in the wonderful state which makes art inevitable." This is what your beliefs and choices do; they create an environment where action is inevitable.

Belief is the conviction to support your actions. Choices fill the space between belief and action. Together, actions, beliefs, and choices turn your ideas into life-size motorized toys — dreams with legs, wheels, and wings.

TRY THIS: PLAY WITH YOUR ABCS

Here is an example of your new ABCs:

- Action: I want to apply for this new job.
- Belief: I would need to believe that I would be seen as a good fit.
- Choice: I choose to believe that I am right for this job and to go for it!

Now try it yourself:

1. *A* is for *action*: I want to _____.
2. *B* is for *belief*: In order to complete this, I would need to believe _____.
3. *C* is for *choice*: I choose to _____.

So now you know your ABCs. Create a habit of checking in with the ABCs often. Before long, anytime you think of an action, the belief and choice will become part of it as well.

Have you ever wondered about the final line in the alphabet song? The one that says, "Next time won't you sing with me?" It doesn't make a lot of sense, especially if everyone in the room is already singing it. Preschoolers are learning that even when they are singing, they are often not heard, which sounds like a great dissertation topic. For the early childhood master's students reading this: you're welcome.

MANIFESTAGRAM
Beliefs and choices = "Be and feel" is so chic!

HAIKOODLE

play as alphabet
a code that everyone knows
it's what we learn first

Don't forget to doodle

9 Play with Creative Blocks

If you could build anything with an infinite set of blocks, what would you build?

Writer's block — or any similar derivative, such as yoga teacher's block or clean-the-kitchen block — is a choice. Whether you say your creativity is blocked or flowing, you are right. The moment you say it, it becomes true. But now you can make some *actual creative blocks* you can use. The ABCs (actions, beliefs, and choices) described in chapter 8 provide the basis of this powerful tool.

TRY THIS: MAKE YOUR ABC BLOCKS

Now we get to have fun! Your set of ABC blocks will be a movable, interactive, three-dimensional map for moving forward. To make your blocks, you can download printable templates at the Artella Land website (see page 48), or you can decorate or embellish any block or cube. You might try wooden or cardboard squares. You could even take a set of baby blocks and paint or draw on them (please don't do this if a baby is actually playing with the blocks, though, because that is just cruel).

To download printable templates, go to: *www.ArtellaLand.com/hsj-downloads.html*

1. Create your A block: Pick six actions that will move you forward. For example, if your goal is to start a blog and publish posts regularly, your block's sides might include steps like creating a name for the blog, deciding on a blog host, and creating a writing schedule.

2. Create your B block: On each side of the block, write a belief that supports your actions — for example, "I believe I have something valuable to contribute" or "I believe that my family will understand that I will want some quiet time for writing."

3. Create your C block: Write six choices in the form "I choose to…" — for example, "I choose to do it differently" or "I choose to have fun and let myself play."

4. Now that you've made your blocks, you get to *play* with them! At any time, simply select one action to set on top of a belief and choice you have selected. This is a really fun ritual and a great way to shake up the act of daily planning. Playing with blocks is so much more fun than looking at a traditional to-do list.

5. For even more play power, partner with synchronicity and use your blocks as dice — literally throw the dice to decide which action you will do next, and which belief and choice will support it.

Hop,
Skip,
Jump

ABC Blocks
Template

an interactive,
three-dimensional
system

Actions
Beliefs
Choices

ACROWHIM
BLOCKS = Build Love: Open, Creative, Kinetic Spirit

HAIKOODLE
play as building blocks
don't worry if they fall down
just create again

10 Making Play Money

FUN FACT: Each standard Monopoly game includes $15,140 in play money. In one year, there is more Monopoly money printed than real money printed throughout the world.

If you were given $15,140 to donate to a charitable cause important to you, what is the first thing that comes to mind? What if you knew you would continue to get $15,140 for charitable giving every week for the rest of your life? Does that change your initial response?

Anxiety about money is often an area in which people get discouraged; their Hopping slows and sometimes even stops altogether. It's hard to enjoy planning and envisioning your dream when pessimistic, defeatist money beliefs stand in the way of possibility. It's helpful to address the money subject sooner rather than later, so that your new beliefs about abundance are built into your entire process. "Play money" isn't just for board games; play can be very useful in changing the way you see money and abundance in your life.

The Story of the *Us* Treasury

In 2003, I hosted Artella's first creative retreat, and about two dozen participants gathered in a wonderful sacred retreat center in Connecticut. The retreat was called "Creative ManiFestival," and the weekend's topic was creative approaches to abundance. We set up a room in the retreat center to be our money-making room and called it the "*Us* Treasury," to represent the fact that this money was created by us. At any time, retreat participants could go into the room and use a variety of art and craft supplies to literally *make* their own money.

Participants then traded their play money with others whenever they felt they had received something meaningful — a word of wisdom, a hug, an idea, heartfelt support. Currency was exchanged in the form of tiny quilts, watercolor splotches, financial quotes written in calligraphy, smiley face stickers, colorful buttons strung with yarn, and so much more.

By the end of the weekend, these women had experienced what it was like to give and receive money with no sense of lack or fear — only joy, appreciation, and fun. They didn't have to worry about running out or receiving too much or not enough. They laughed and sighed as they made money, gave it away, made more, and played more.

TRY THIS: MAKING MONEY

1. Identify a belief you would like to have about money.
2. Design a new kind of money to reflect this belief. Sketch the new design, or use any materials you like to make it.
3. As you design your money, here are some things to ponder:

   How might the world be different if everyone used this kind of money?

   How might you integrate these insights into your own sense of abundance?

   What is play money's message to you?

4. Give a piece of your money away. Leave it where someone can find it. Give it to a friend. Send it along with your check when paying your bills. Give it to the teller at the bank with a big smile.*

---

* Acceptance of this deposit is not guaranteed, but a feeling of complete and utter joy and silliness is.

HAIKOODLE

play as golden coins
most valuable things we own
the riches of life

11 Crayonstorming for New Ideas

FUN FACT: Samuel Allen invented the Flexible Flyer — the classic steel-runner sled — in 1900 when he wanted to develop a product that could be manufactured during the nonfarming months, to persuade workers at his seasonal farm equipment company against migrating south during winter. He got his idea while paging through the dictionary, when his eyes landed on the word *sled*.

Grab a dictionary, or any book,
and let your eye land on any random word.
How might this word add new possibilities to your dreams?

My husband, Tony, loves brainstorming, planning, and everything in between. It's where he is most invigorated, enjoying his natural strength. Years ago, during our long-distance courtship, I was considering moving to be closer to where he lived, so I took a trip to visit him. He was looking forward to gathering maps, exploring neighborhoods, and collecting newspapers for possible job opportunities for me. He was in awe when, by the end of my second day on the visit, I had gotten a job, found an apartment, and was ready to sign my lease. In retrospect, I can see how his brainstorming and planning might have helped me make even better decisions than I made by Jumping on my own. But he also learned that effective action doesn't *always* need a lot of planning either. Let's just say we are very lucky that we have one another to balance our very extreme inclinations. When it comes to manifesting, we're a good pair of coconuts.

The Trouble with Brainstorming

In *Play: How It Shapes the Brain, Opens the Imagination, and Invigorates the Soul*, Stuart Brown talks about brainstorming in corporate environments: "When it is going well, brainstorming is also play.... The problem, I think, is that some brainstorming sessions never become playful. Although no one is supposed to criticize, some group members will feel that unspoken criticism is in the air. Or a kind of unspoken hierarchy hampers the freedom of expression." Brown shares a story of consulting for a company experiencing this kind of stilted brainstorming; his solution was to invite the team to play a game of Twister before the brainstorming began, to make sure that a playful atmosphere had been created, allowing creative ideas to flow.

Similar challenges can also come up when brainstorming solo. Some people reenact the dynamics mentioned above with themselves, as they judge and criticize each idea they come up with. Given that it is quite difficult to play Twister with oneself, we need to create another solution to keep brainstorming playful.

TRY THIS: PUTTING A NEW BOX OF CRAYONS TO WORK

1. If you don't already have them, buy a box of crayons and a coloring book. Dollar stores are great for this purpose, but you can feel free to purchase crayons at a high-end department store if you prefer, especially if you are using play money (see chapter 10 on play money).

2. Use your crayons and coloring book to purposely, intentionally, color outside the lines. Scribble. Break the crayons in half and smash them into the page. Write in the margins of the coloring book. This is your warm-up, to see what it feels like to break the rules, remember what it feels like to hold these waxy small cylinders in your

hands, experiment with darker and lighter shades as you color, and follow the unmistakable scent of crayons back to a childhood memory.

3. After your warm-up is complete, write down a question for which you'd like to see some new possibilities.

4. Pick one color, and use it to write down words that rhyme with the color's name. For example, if you picked up a blue crayon, you'd write words that rhyme with *blue* (like *zoo*, *goo*, *shoe*, and *cockatoo*). Repeat for other colors, making new lists of rhyming words. I will save you time by letting you know in advance that there isn't much that truly rhymes with *orange*.

5. Use the lists of words to inspire answers to your question. Begin by using a crayon to write, "Maybe I could _____." Then refer back to the lists of rhyming words to tickle your imagination, and write down all the wild and crazy ideas that come to mind. As you write, change colors whenever you like. Notice if the color you are using changes the flavor of the ideas in any way. How are pink ideas different from green ideas?

6. Now you have an imaginative list of all kinds of ideas that you've pulled from unusual places, and you can sift through your colorful lists to find notions that might benefit from further exploration.

ACROWHIM
IDEAS = Invade Daring Evolutionary Areas Soon

HAIKOODLE

play as red crayon
the one that is used the most
worn down, but still works

12 Finding a Playmate

Who was your best friend as a child, and what was most meaningful about the friendship? What might those memories tell you about the kind of support you need right now?

S hortly after becoming engaged to the man of my dreams, I read about the mating habits of monarch butterflies. When they mate, *they carry each other*. Sometimes the male carries the female, and sometime the female carries the male. Because that is an apt metaphor for our relationship, Tony and I included a butterfly release during our casual outdoor wedding. It was a whimsical touch on a gorgeous day, except for the very unfortunate story of the butterflies who got too much sun and, sadly, turned into baked butterflies. Trust me, young lovers, you don't want overheated butterflies at your wedding. But the symbolism of the kind of mutual support we offer each other — sometimes I carry him, somctimes he carries me — remains in flight.

The Different Types of Playmate

One of the most important aspects of the Hop phase is to cultivate relationships and enhanced experiences of personal support. In child development, various kinds of social play are identified as being important. You can use the following definitions to inspire the types of supportive play that you'll need in the beginning stages of a dream:

Rough-and-tumble playmates. You need playmates who will roll around with you as you toss and tumble with new ideas. Make sure you are selecting people you trust and who do not bring negativity or discouraging energy to the table. My friend Dan is a good example of a "rough-and-tumble" playmate. I can go to him with creative ideas, and he adds fabulous feedback and offers new ideas in a way that is fun and delightful.

Belonging playmates. You need playmates who are familiar with what you are experiencing and can serve as great examples to both normalize and inspire your process. My friend Tama fits the bill for this one. She and I have so many similar professional experiences that a conversation with her is the perfect place for me to take a deep breath and feel that I am understood and really known. It's well documented that children need "parallel play" experiences, where they feel safe playing *next* to another child, though not necessarily with them. We need that, too.

Celebratory playmates. You need playmates who can be your cheerleaders, champions, and celebrants. These friends may or may not have a direct interest in or connection to what you're working on, but they'll be there to cheer you on. Jean E. is a friend who celebrates with me no matter what. Our initial bond was built around our roles of mothering young kids, but if I have a professional accomplishment, she'll want to take me out for a celebratory pedicure.

TRY THIS: HAVE A TEA PARTY

Take a look at the playmates in your life. Who currently fits into the categories of rough-and-tumble playmate, belonging playmate, and celebratory playmate? Where are the empty spaces, and how might you fill them?

After you have identified those who provide support, use your crayons to draw a picture of *all* of you coming together for an imaginary tea party. Add details to your drawing to make it come alive. Add decorations, a menu, and other elements. Think about whether your tea party might have a theme: Is it a marathon-training tea party? A business-building tea party? A new-apartment tea party? Do any made-up *tea* words — *abilitea, creativitea, believabilitea* — spark ideas?

MANIFESTAGRAM

"Say, Say, My Playmate" = May my easy pal stay?

HAIKOODLE

play as a best friend
join me for a sleepover
see you in my dreams

13 Imaginary Friends

Did you have an imaginary friend as a child?
If so, invite this old friend for a visit; if not,
invent an imaginary friend who could help you out today.

Children use imaginary friends for many reasons, often to fill important roles or empty spots in their lives. My son, Kai, has introduced a number of baby aliens to our household, each of them wanting to be adopted, and I assume this is his way of working through his feelings about being an only child. I'm glad they are invisible, or we'd run out of room pretty quickly!

Where Do Imaginary Friends Hang Out?

Adults can create imaginary friends, too! Inspiring people whom you've never met can step into those roles that, right now, may not be filled by living, breathing people in your life. When I read Stephen Sondheim's autobiography, *Finishing the Hat*, I was comforted and inspired by learning about his creative process. He will, most likely, never be an in-person playmate, but just knowing he is there inspires me to go deeper into my own creative process. He is an imaginary friend who is a belonging playmate (see chapter 12 for the different types of playmate). If any reader happens to know Mr. Sondheim and would like to make an introduction, please feel free.

My buddy Jill Badonsky wrote an awesome book about the power of imaginary friends, *The Nine Modern-Day Muses (and a Bodyguard)*. The book introduces ten muses who function as our imaginary friends and whom we can call on as needed. One inspiration for her muses is characters in movies. In a class we taught together, she shared this example with the students:

> I'm a movie buff and I find that characters in movies really can empower me. When I watched the movie *Fargo*, the character of Marge immediately became one of my heroes because she was such an empowered person. Even though she was pregnant, dealing with incompetent deputies and uncooperative people, she just got right to the point and got things done. She didn't go into a victim mode or create any drama. She just went straight to getting things done. This is what we need in the creative process. That's how Marge became my get-it-done Muse.

TRY THIS: YOUR IMAGINARY BOARD OF DIRECTORS

1. Make a list of some imaginary friends who could fill the roles you need (to review from chapter 12, think of rough-and-tumble playmates, belonging playmates, and celebratory playmates). Pull from famous people, important figures from history, friends or family members who have passed away, or, following Jill's lead, use movie characters.

2. Create a visual of your imaginary friends. This can be as simple as drawing a circle of stick figures who represent

these people. It could also be a collage, a painting, or faces within a digital greeting card.

3. Using this visual, call a meeting of the board of directors of your life. This is similar to designing your dream dinner party, where you put together a fantasy dinner party in which the possibilities for guests are unlimited. But this time, you don't have to worry about what Brad Pitt and Joan of Arc might be doing in the corner, because you're putting your guests to work. Ask them about your current challenges. What would they say? How might they help? Write your discoveries on your artwork or in your journal.

> ACROWHIM
> FRIEND = Finding Reason Inside
> Energizing New Dialogue

HAIKOODLE
play as my buddy
who lives only in my brain
knowing me the best

14 The Superhero Phase

What would you like your superpower to be, and how would you use it?

When Kai went through his superhero phase, as many little boys do, he latched onto Spiderman as his favorite. This distressed me greatly, as I'd had an irrational fear of Spiderman since childhood. I have no idea where it came from, but I know my older sister — who was my earliest playmate — used to taunt me about it. I am now proudly recovered from this phobia, due to the extreme immersion therapy I received during Kai's Spiderman obsession. At the height of this phase, Kai recycled a couple of red mesh bags that had held oranges, and wrapped them around his legs as part of his Spiderman costume for Halloween. Yes, my son paraded around the neighborhood in red plastic fishnet stockings. His father was so proud.

Picking the Superhero That's Right for You

For a long time, my superhero icon was Wonder Woman. I'm not alone. A teleclass I taught titled "Discover Your Inner Wonder Woman" had over a thousand people sign up, so there are a lot of us Wonder Woman wannabes running around. However, not long ago, I realized that Wonder Woman was no longer the right superhero for me. Her satin short-shorts were just a bit too tight, her schedule a bit too busy, her hair a little too coiffed, her codependency a little too obvious when the comic word balloon exclaimed, "I am who the world needs me to be. I'm Wonder Woman."

So I settled on Glinda the Good Witch from *The Wizard of Oz* as my new superhero. Instead of running to save the day, Glinda gracefully glides in and out of a magic bubble when she is needed. Instead of forcefully throwing a magic lasso, she waves her sparkly magic wand with the slightest twist of her wrist. When I have a problem, I think, "WWGD?" (that's "What would Glinda do?"), and it helps me see a new solution.

MY SUPERHERO MAKEOVER

This transformation became even more powerful when I picked up my markers. Looking at my transformation through an artistic lens rather than a practical one, I was delighted to see that my Wonder Woman could turn into my Glinda with just a few small tweaks. Playing with the illustration helped me see that my attitudes and choices could also be shifted with ease. Here are the "before" and "after" images:

1. Think about your dream, vision, or goal. What would you like to change about your current situation? What kinds of support do you need?

2. Imagine a superhero who could do anything you need. What would you want him or her to do, and what helps him or her do this? Is it an inherent superpower or maybe a magic accessory? For example, you might like a superhero who has a magic manicure that instantly repels criticism. Or perhaps you'd like to try some "yes-ray" vision to help you remain optimistic when you get frustrated.

3. How might you incorporate some of these superpowers into your own life? Using the examples above, you could treat yourself to a "magic manicure" to boost your self-esteem, or write the word "yes" on the inside of your glasses. As a bonus, if you write "yes" where others can see it, it will look like "sey" to them. This will result in many conversations beginning with the inquiry "Does that say 'sey'?" which inevitably will lead to confused laughter. When playfully manifesting a meaningful life, laughter is a great superpower to have.

MANIFESTAGRAM
Selecting a new superhero =
Cleaning our sweet sphere

HAIKOODLE

play as Superman
it's a bird, it's a plane, it's...
anything I want

TOP TEN SIGNS YOUR CHILD (OR INNER CHILD) IS GOING THROUGH A SUPERHERO PHASE

10. Your laundry consists primarily of capes.
9. You find yourself ducking imaginary bats.
8. Your child sounds wisely metaphorical when using "kryptonite" in a sentence.
7. Neighbors have expressed concern over seeing your child repeatedly on the roof.
6. At a grown-up dinner party, you initiate conversations about the gaps in gender and racial representation in the superhero universe.
5. When asking a friend for advice about the paint color for your kitchen, you casually use the terms "Green Goblin green" and "Joker blazer purple" as plausible options.
4. The sight of family members sleeping upside down doesn't faze you.
3. You actually know how fast a speeding bullet travels.
2. You get highly suspicious when your seemingly normal co-worker spends a little too long in the bathroom.
1. When sharing recent photos with a friend, you are asked, "Was this from Halloween?" and you reply, "No, Tuesday."

15 Playful Permission Slips

FUN FACT: According to the American Association of School Administrators, more than half of U.S. schools eliminated at least some planned field trips in 2010–11.

If you could go on a field trip to learn something new, where would you go?

I remember the old permission slips we took home from school for upcoming field trips. They included carbon paper — certainly the messiest office supply ever to exist — so that my mom could sign it and keep a copy for herself, which actually doesn't make a lot of sense. I can't think of a reason she would need a copy, unless it was to assist her in appearing to be interested while halfway listening to the school-day anecdotes shared over dinner. With this system, the savvy mom could simply go to her trusty file cabinet and see if there was a permission slip for that day; upon finding one, she would instantly know whether her child's story is about a visit to the zoo or to city hall, which is, after all, an important distinction.

Waiting for Permission

Taking your time in the Hop stage offers you the opportunity to identify and fully address any areas that might be holding you back from taking action. For example, are you waiting for *permission* to do what you want to do? For many of us, the power of permission dates back to childhood, when we looked to parents, authority figures, and carbon copies for permission. Is any part of you waiting for permission to move forward?

Resurrecting permission slips — without the carbon paper — is a great way to put your conviction into writing, and many of us find it easier to believe something when we see it written down. I recommend two resources for fun, playful permission slips: *Living Juicy*, by SARK, which is full of permission slips to be creative; and *Permission Slips...for Your Heart & Soul*, by Patricia J. Mosca, which includes the most colorful, artsy permission slips I've ever seen — ready to cut out and give to yourself whenever you need them.

Imagine you have been given a permission slip containing the words you need most right now. What does it say? Do you need to give yourself permission to break the rules and do things in a new way? Permission to trade security for happiness? Permission to shatter other people's ideas about your life? Permission to put a walrus in your hair? (Just making sure you're paying attention.) Do you need to give yourself permission to fail, to believe in yourself, to start over?

TRY THIS: A TALE OF TWO PERMISSION SLIPS

1. Think of a permission statement that would summarize the kind of personal permission you need right now. Draw a rectangle, and write your statement in the middle of it.

2. Make a second version of your slip, this time making it more playful. You can use these questions to spark ideas:

   How could you make your permission slip colorful?
   How could you make your permission slip silly?
   How could you make it three-dimensional?
   How could you make your permission slip into a song?

3. Look at your two slips. You have permission to choose the one that is most motivating for you and to decide if you'd like to use carbon paper to replicate it. If you choose the playful option, congratulations — you are playing well with your manifesting self. If you choose the initial unembellished one...well, I'm giving *myself* permission to persevere and get your linear mind playing! Let's keep going!

> ACROWHIM
> SLIP = Speaking Love Inspires Permission

HAIKOODLE

play as permission
I don't even have to ask
life gave it to me

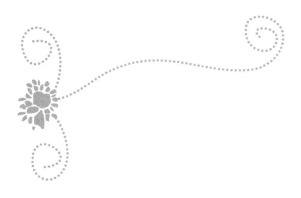

16 **Your Mission Paintment**

FUN FACT: Jenga, the name of the popular stacking game, means "build it" in Swahili.

Imagine you are building your ideal life.
If you could use any materials in the world, what would you use?

The phrase "If you build it, he will come" holds a lot of energy in the Hop phase. In the film *Field of Dreams*, it was the voice that Kevin Costner's character heard whispered whenever he visited the field. It was the voice he listened to whenever he faced doubts.

When you think of "If you build it, he will come," what is *your* "it"? What are *you* building? Organizations, companies, and businesses have mission statements to clarify what they want to build. Contemporary personal development books encourage us to write a mission statement to encompass who we are and what we want to create.

In the interests of total self-disclosure, a mission statement is one of the aspects of the Hop phase where I roll my eyes and get a little bored. Somehow, the very term *mission statement* and its usage in our society feel so serious. The term also implies there is something *finite* about a mission. As my client Judy said, "I'm afraid to write a mission statement because then it's *official*. Then I can't change it."

What if a mission statement could be playful? What if your mission, like you, could be ever evolving, ever changing, and always expanding? While a mission statement can feel intimidating or limiting, you can try a "mission *paintment*": a spontaneous work of art that expresses your vision with bold colors, wild strokes, and evolving designs.

TRY THIS: BUILD YOUR BILLBOARD

1. Think of a very well-traveled area where many, many people would be likely to see a billboard. If the first thing that comes to mind is the route from your door to the sidewalk, I'm assuming you don't get out much, so you will need to stretch your imagination a bit in order to do this exercise.

2. Pretend you get to paint a message on a billboard in that area, to be seen by those many, many people. Try these prompts to explore what it might say:

    I really want to tell people _____.
    This is important to me because _____.
    My message for the world reads: _____.
    When it comes right down to it, I am here to _____.

    What do your answers reveal about your mission?

3. What is one way you might express your mission this week? You are welcome to rent a billboard and one of those crazy-tall billboard ladders to make your own billboard, or you could try something a bit more simple, like making a playful sign with your statement or saying it out loud before you go to sleep. However, if you are prone to sleepwalking, please do not try the first suggestion, as you may be putting yourself in danger. Studies show that billboard assemblers are almost always awake.

MANIFESTAGRAM

Mission paintment = Inmost spin: name it!

HAIKOODLE

play as juicy paint
ready to splatter and drip
living as fine art

{ Don't forget to doodle }

17   Playing Dress-Up

FUN FACT: During the 1953 coronation of Queen Elizabeth II, Madame Alexander commemorated the event by dressing thirty-six dolls in historically accurate costumes made with cloth from the same mill that produced the original clothes.

If a doll production company made a doll representation of you, what would it be wearing, and what accessories would be included?

y dear friend Tama Kieves wrote a brilliant book called *Inspired & Unstoppable: Wildly Succeeding in Your Life's Work!*, and in it, shared a story that touches on the ever-changing nature of both confidence and fashion trends. When she first left Harvard Law School to follow her dream of becoming a writer, she bought a three-piece purple silk pantsuit at a Goodwill store and hung it in her closet. It represented everything she thought she wanted to be: the published author and inspirational speaker who was confident in success, speaking to throngs of people, and doing it all in a purple suit.

Dressing the Part

The suit remained in Tama's closet for years, representing her half-lived dream. I love how she describes finally donating the suit back to a thrift store: "Finally, the outfit became ridiculous. It was the poster child of another decade, with square shoulders that looked like shelves for books and trophies or maybe some handy built-in platforms, just in case you might want to accessorize with a pair of parrots." Personally, I love the idea of accessorizing with a pair of parrots. If I pare it down, I'd feed pears to my pairs of parrots. But back to Tama's story: She donated the suit, kept on with her dream, and eventually found herself with a bestselling book, speaking all over the country. She was not wearing the purple suit, but she was living her dream. The purple suit fulfilled its purpose, though; Tama realized that the girl who bought the suit *believed* she would get there, and if that girl hadn't let her imagination "play dress-up," it wouldn't have happened.

Children play dress-up to expand their imaginations and try different roles. In the Hop phase, you get to focus on figuring out who you are and who you want to be. In the ARTbundance Certification Training program, we teach that even when using the phone to coach clients or teach classes, it makes a huge difference to dress as we would if we were meeting a client or an audience in person. Doing so changes the way we carry ourselves and does wonders for confidence. I admit that I do not always follow this advice, as I love working in my pj's. But then again, I've been known to go out in the world in my pj's, too, so perhaps I'm just being consistent.

For similar reasons, I encourage clients to order a short run of business cards — or, as the Victorians called them, "calling cards" — to try different aspects of their dream. Creating a calling card boldly declares your dream and allows it to be real. Whether you hand the card to another person isn't important — especially when you are happily Hopping. This card takes something you already know about yourself and puts it in writing. Think of it this way: we all hold an *energetic* calling card in our pocket. We all have a way of saying who we are, even to strangers. At the park this week, I could read the energetic calling cards of the other parents on the playground: "social butterfly," "genuine smile," "curious and quiet." We all carry around energetic credentials that show who we are.

TRY THIS: CREATE YOUR CALLING CARD

1. Make a list of words that describe you. Don't think about this too much; just write the first things that come to mind.

2. Make your list "official" by giving yourself some credentials. Add *postnominal* letters to your name — which, as of about twenty seconds ago, I am qualified to say is the correct term for those fancy initials that appear after a professional's name. For example, I have met Judy, a PhD (passionate, hilarious diva); Bill, an MHAPM (master of heart art and purple moose); and Alisson, an RWPG (rolling-with-the-punches genius).

3. Now play dress-up. What new qualities would you like to try out, and what are the initials to designate this expertise? Feel free to add lots of initials, just like the fancy people do. I found literally hundreds of official postnominal letters on *Wikipedia*, so, by golly, you can have as many as you want. You can even make a whole deck of calling cards and keep them in your wallet so you can "dress up" at will and have lots of choices at your disposal.

ACROWHIM
DRESS UP = Do Radical Experimental Stuff;
See Unique Potential

HAIKOODLE

play as a ball gown
satin, organza, and tulle
swishing as I dance

18 — Design Your Plan-it-arium

FUN FACT: The David Crowder Band used over seven hundred thousand vintage Lite-Brite pegs to create a stop-motion-animation music video called "SMS Shine." It took 2,150 hours and 148 pizzas.

If you could spell a word or phrase using stars in the sky, what would you spell?

One day, little Kai was listening to me and Tony talk about the plan for the day. Likely focused on his then-current outer-space obsession, he said, "You know what you need, Mommy? A *plan-it*-arium — you know, instead of a planetarium!" His fascination with wordplay makes me wonder if it's a genetic trait and worry that he might work me out of a job.

A Playful Approach to Planning

If I told you this chapter was about *planning*, I imagine you would have a very distinct reaction. Most people either love making plans or detest it. Some may enjoy making long-range plans but resist making a plan for a daily structure, while for others, the very opposite is true. One thing is certain: society tells us that we "should" have a plan, whether we want to or not.

We are constantly bombarded with messages about planning.

In order to save time, we need to microplan our days on our favorite digital device. In order to spend our lives well, we need to have five-year, ten-year, and twenty-year plans. The news is full of reports about health plans, financial plans, and political plans. Everywhere you look, you get a message: *plans are important*, and so you need to have one, or perhaps fourteen, right now.

This approach to planning does not sound like a lot of fun, so I know I won't be doing it. Taking inspiration from Kai, let's try a playful way to plan that is solar powered by star stuff.

TRY THIS: YOUR PLAN-IT-ARY MAP

Follow the steps below to create your plan-it-ary map. Refer to the sidebar for further guidance.

1. Draw a circle, and in the center, write your planned intention: "My plan is to _____." This is *your* plan-it.
2. Draw and label the sun(s). A sun is the closest light source, and it symbolizes the thing that gives you the most light — what makes you twinkle, light up, illuminate, shine, shimmer. (And who knew there were so many synonyms for the things that suns do so well?)
3. Draw and label the moon(s). A moon represents the mystical, magical forces — such as a higher power, trust, faith, your muse, alien life, or Superman — that support you in your plan.
4. Identify and add any black holes. Black holes are stars that have died out, and they represent the things that are no longer needed or relevant to your plan — things like old beliefs, memories, experiences, clutter, outdated systems, and expired items in your refrigerator.
5. Identify and add the dark matter. While black holes can be detected in space — they respond to frequencies and light that shines around them — dark matter *cannot* be detected, as it completely stops the sun. In this map, dark matter represents the deepest, perhaps unspoken, fear about your plan, the biggest core fear that could hold

you back. You might try this phrase to help you reach it: "Deep down, where nobody knows it but me, I am afraid of _____."

6. Identify and add the orbiting objects. It has been said that we are the sum total of the three people with whom we spend the most time. Place the people with whom you spend the most time in orbit around your plan-it. These days, as I've been spending lots of time writing in a local café, I think those three people would be the head barista on the morning, afternoon, and evening shifts. All seem to be nice people, so that is good news. Next, near the orbiting objects, add a birthing star: one person whom you'd like to bring into your orbit in a more prominent way. For me, this might be my massage therapist.

7. Discover the wormhole, and add it to the map. A wormhole is a hypothetical tunnel between the present and some other place in the space-time continuum. In quantum physics, the wormhole is our vehicle for time travel, our access to parallel universes, and our connection to the multiverse. On this map, *your* wormhole is a tube or tunnel in which your dream is already a reality. At the end of the wormhole, write some phrases that describe what will happen when your plan comes to pass: How do you feel? What are you doing? Who or what is around you?

8. Study your plan-it-ary map. You have just mapped out the most important cosmic components in the universe of your life as you know it. They also correspond to the elements that are important to the process of manifesting anything. Pick one insight from this exercise that brings you a little closer to the truth of your vision, and write it down in your calendar or daily planner, as a reminder for frequent reflection. When you tap into the power of play, even the alien concept of planning gets to sparkle and shine!

SAMPLE PLAN-IT-ARY MAP

Here's a sample map to help you follow the instructions in Try This: Your Plan-it-ary Map. You can also download a full-size printable map at the Artella Land website.

To download printable map, go to:
www.ArtellaLand.com/hsj-downloads.html

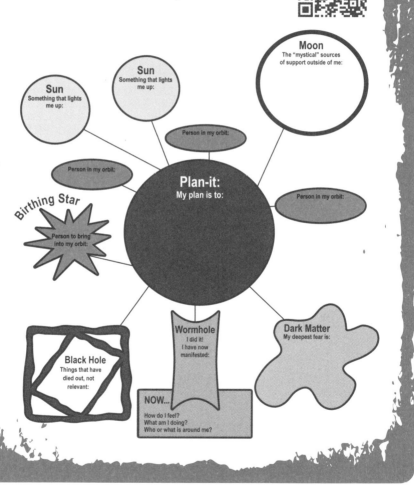

HAIKOODLE

play as the night sky
shining bright light years away
long ago, but close

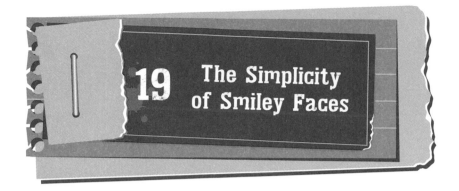

19 The Simplicity of Smiley Faces

FUN FACT: Though the identity of the original designer of the traditional smiley face logo is disputed, one way the image was introduced into popular culture was through a 1962 marketing campaign for a New York radio station. Listeners were invited to answer their phone saying, "WMCA good guys!" in order to win a sweatshirt with a smiley face.

Imagine that you could share some joy every time
you answered the phone. What might you say?

A few years ago, I was looking for new eyeglass frames, and I spent an hour in the shop, trying on different options. I finally found a pair that, when I tried them on, made my face look like *me*. I was happy to have finally made a choice, until my husband pointed out that they were *exactly* the same frames I already had. Here I had spent an hour looking for new frames, only to discover that I already had what I wanted. I discovered that my face already looked like me.

Does Your Face Look Like You?

When you allow yourself to lie back, relax, and think about your dream, what happens to your face? Does a shy little smile break out over your lips? Do you fall into laughter? Does your brow crinkle as you worry about the details? Do you roll your eyes in doubt, perhaps even unconsciously?

What happens to your face when you are thinking of your dream is really important. This is literally the "face" of your creative dream, and it can give you helpful clues. For example, when your face is lit up, pay attention — this is what you need to be doing *more* of as you take steps forward. On the other hand, when your face is tight or constricted, this is where you need to find new support and solutions. I tell my clients that when they come up with a name for a business or a product, if they don't *smile* when they say it, they haven't found the right name yet. Unless we are characters in a sci-fi film, our face is always with us. Becoming more aware of its clues is a helpful way to have an instant gauge on what's working and what's not.

TRY THIS: FACING YOUR DREAM

1. Think of an area of your dream that is feeling stuck or stale. Hint: if your brow is furrowed when you think of it, you've probably landed on the right thing.

2. Go on a scavenger hunt to look for faces in unusual places. Bring a sketchbook to draw them. Faces are everywhere. Here are some ideas to get you started:

   Faces in nature: trees, flowers, clouds
   Faces on surfaces: floors, walls, ceilings, pavement
   Faces in food: fruits, potato skins, muffins

3. When you see a face that looks like it is smiling, write in your journal, "This face wants me to know _____." Pay attention to the surroundings and see if there are any clues or ideas that might help you solve your problem.

As you start looking for more and more smiling faces in abstract places, you will start being more aware of your own face. Your face becomes the measurement of how your dream is moving forward. The more you smile, the more beautiful you are!

Maybe you'll get discovered by someone who says you oughta be in pictures! Or even better, you might just get discovered by yourself.

ACROWHIM

SMILE = Small Movements Inspire Love Everywhere

HAIKOODLE

play as a big smile
tiny muscles work as one
exercise often

20 Primary Colors

FUN FACT: In 2008, Hasbro gave a makeover to the popular mystery game Clue. The characters were given first names and backstories, but the last names continued to refer to colors: Mr. Green, Mrs. White, Colonel Mustard, Miss Scarlett, Mrs. Peacock, and Professor Plum.

When you think of your vision or dream,
what color comes to mind, and why?

I n *Winnie the Pooh*, A.A. Milne has Pooh give Ecyore a "Useful Pot to put things in" as a birthday gift. For those of you who gravitate toward the Hop phase, this would, indeed, be an ideal gift. People who naturally enjoy Hopping will either spend a good deal of time organizing or wish they did. They relish the opportunity to look at and design things that support what I think of as *systemic health*: the state of environments and systems in our lives. Those of us who — like me! — *aren't* naturally drawn to sorting, clearing, and de-cluttering need to find a playful way to enter into the activity, like organizing things by color.

Making Organization Playful with Color

One of my favorite tricks for making organization more playful is to use colors. A painter's palette, the sweet pans in a child's watercolor set, shelves of paint samples in the home improvement store...now *these* are images of organization that make me very happy. I love to look at the rows of paint samples and just imagine what it would be like if life could be that orderly *and* that colorful.

If you also love the look of organized colors, you can use that to help you feel more playful when doing organizational tasks. It can be very calming to sort things by colors — book spines, bottles of paint, dishes in the dishwasher, boxes in the pantry. Color-driven organization will get you to focus on any systemic task — organization, clearing, de-cluttering — with a touch of fun.

If I have to organize my financial records and receipts, lemme tell you, it's *not* going to happen. Or if it does, it will involve bodily threats and many, many doughnuts. However, if I *start* by sorting the receipts in colorful file folders, I will be *far* more likely to keep the momentum to finish the job. Colors can even help me organize the ideas in my head. I once was trying to write an article called "Business Blueprints for Creative Entrepreneurs," and I couldn't get a word out. When I changed it to "Playing with Passionate Purpleprints," the thing practically wrote itself. Where could *your* dream use a bit of color?

TRY THIS: ORGANIZATIONAL PALETTE PLAY

Use these prompts to explore ways that color might help you gain some momentum in planning and organization:

- What role does color play in your life?
- What is your favorite color, and why?
- What memories do you have about favorite colors as a kid?
- What color do you associate with your dream or project?
- What needs to be organized, sorted, or de-cluttered right now? How might *color* make this task become more playful and fun?

MANIFESTAGRAM	
Colorful organization = Training a colorful zoo	

HAIKOODLE

play as a rainbow
painted across a big sky
divinity games

21   Playing House

FUN FACT: The Treehotel in Sweden offers high-design accommodations with a touch of play: guests stay in a collection of tree rooms designed by Scandinavia's leading architects.

Imagine the ideal tree house where you could rest, recharge, and rejuvenate your dream. What are some of its amenities?

No matter where we consider home to be, perhaps nothing influences our general mood and productivity more than our environment. In *The Re-enchantment of Everyday Life*, Thomas Moore writes: "Nothing is more intimate than home, and therefore nothing more proper to the soul. Whatever it takes to call forth the spirits of home, our own lares and penates — ancient Roman household spirits — is worth our effort and expense. It is always time to trim a plant, glaze a window, clean a rug, or write a poem about home."

Feeling at Home

The desire to have a comfortable space to relax is a very basic one. Members of the animal kingdom are motivated by the same innate desire: to create nests and other comfortable, functional shelters. Does your home provide exactly what your dream needs?

Or do you put up mental blinders to cover up the clutter and uninspiring decor in your living space? Play to the rescue!

Candy Land is one of the most popular games of all time, and it has withstood the test of time because the idea of living in a "candy land" is the ultimate fantasy for many children. What is *your* ultimate fantasy? What is the most *playful* environment you could live in? What if you lived at Disney World? On the beach? In a tree house? In outer space?

A fantasy of mine is to live within a formal garden, like the ones I have visited in England. I love to imagine that I could live in row upon row of endless flowers. So colorful and yet so organized, but not in a boring way. I imagine bringing into my estate a housecleaning crew of fairies who would tend to everything and make my bed of roses each morning.

Select your own fantasy land, and then follow the instructions below.

TRY THIS: FIND YOUR FANTASY LAND

1. Walk through your living space and see if there's an area, even just a small one, that could use a little bit of play. Think about the corners where a little smile could go a long way. As you see some possibilities, make note of them.

2. How might you incorporate some items from your fantasy land into your home? For example, to carry out my garden fantasy, I might replace the serious coffee table books with floral-themed coloring books or make some pipe cleaner flowers to go in a tiny vase on a kitchen shelf.

3. What about the spaces outside your living space? Where else do you spend time? The inside of my car is decorated with plastic orange, yellow, and white flowers, and it truly makes a difference as I drive around. And every time I go through a drive-through, I get compliments on it. I call it my "carden," my traveling garden, which takes me exactly where I need to go — straight to play!

HAIKOODLE

play as a cabin
cozy quilts on all the beds
peace within the walls

TOP TEN SIGNS IT'S TIME TO CLEAN HOUSE

10. You now put on a pair of boots before entering.
9. You've turned to naming parts of your room after famous mountain ranges.
8. You're hearing rumors that the plants are trying to hatch an escape plan.
7. Even dust is having a hard time finding a clean nook to land on.
6. Your wastebasket hasn't been seen for weeks.
5. Your friends and family have given each room a nickname with the word *pit* in it.
4. You've begun to tell yourself, "Who needs to sit down anyway?"
3. You invite guests to "shimmy on in."
2. It takes you more time to find something than it does to just go buy a new one.
1. Visitors are asking when your thrift store is opening.

22   The Memory Game

FUN FACT: Simon — the electronic memory game that was popular in the 1970s and 1980s — featured tones from a major triad resembling a trumpet fanfare.

*Recall the moment when you first got a glimpse
of your dream, perhaps without even realizing what it was.
Imagine you are telling the story, sharing all the specifics
with full fanfare and finesse. What details would you include?*

My mother recently moved out of the house in which she had lived for thirty-eight years, the house where I grew up. A new, lovely family has moved into the house, and they have completely remodeled it. During the move, I had a really weird dream that I had sneaked into the house, while the new family was asleep, and disconnected their light fixtures. Not long after, in real, honest-to-goodness life, I was invited inside to see their new updates one day when I just happened to be standing in their front yard. This is not as bad as it sounds; I was visiting my friend who lives across the street. Really — I promise!

At any rate, though the structure of the house looked entirely different — I could still feel the memories everywhere, as if a fairy with a slide projector were playing games with me, casting images on walls, floors, bedspreads, dinner plates. Some were hazy, some were clear, some I'm not sure were even real. The house still holds memories.

Collecting Memories

What are your childhood memories of play? What did you play with, and whom did you play with? You may have lots of memories of childhood play or very few, if any. If you experienced an unhappy childhood, this question might be difficult, so be gentle with yourself as you look into your past.

I love these words from Fred Rogers — a.k.a. Mister Rogers: "When we treat children's play as seriously as it deserves, we are helping them feel the joy that's to be found in the creative spirit. It's the things we play with and the people who help us play that make a great difference in our lives."

Tapping into the places and spaces where you played as a child makes it easier to connect with play *now*, as you are using it to buoy your productivity and manifest your meaningful life. Remembering your favorite toys, games, and collections is a great way to exercise your play muscles.

TRY THIS: A TRIP DOWN MEMORY LANE

Answer these questions in your journal, preferably with your crayons:

- What did you love to do as a child?
- What did you collect as a child? Baseball cards? Barbies? Rocks? Bugs? Pennies? What do you remember about these collections? How did you store these collections?
- Was there a toy or game that you wanted but never had? What made it so attractive and desirable to you?
- Did you prefer playing by yourself or with others?

Take a look at your responses. How are your memories related to your experiences right now? What insights might you take away from this trip down memory lane?

HAIKOODLE

play as memory
blurry but still part of me
it knows who I am

23 Your Inner Child's Bag of Toys

If you had one wish for all the children of the world, what would it be? Is this wish related to an experience from your own childhood? How does pinpointing this wish support your own dream today?

My friend Dan Gremminger is a talented artist who offers a truly unique artistic service called "Lost Toys by Danno." It begins with a questionnaire in which the client shares memories about a favorite toy. If photos are available, Dan uses them, but he will also work from descriptions or perhaps the client's simple sketch. He then creates a painting of the toy against a backdrop of vintage comics. In a brochure about the service, Dan writes, "My goal is to give this companion from childhood the royal portrait treatment, in its gently worn and much-loved condition. Whether these beloved friends still exist or have been lost to time, this is the opportunity to honor a Lost Toy with an original and personalized work of art."

I was the recipient of a Lost Toy portrait when I was in a lengthy recovery period after a spinal tap that went terribly wrong. When Dan unveiled his portrait of "Chickie" — my long-gone stuffed friend — I felt comforted, alive, and equipped to heal myself, like that little girl who held on to Chickie when she was in the hospital as a child. Chickie's message to me when I needed her most was: You are safe. You are not alone. Hold on tight to me.

Talking to Your Toys

As you are preparing to move out of the Hop phase in order to Skip and Jump in your adventure, imagine that you can gather a bag of tools to help. The first thing to put in the bag is, naturally, *toys*! Think of toys you loved from your childhood and a message those toys might bring you today. Here are a few examples from a recent workshop:

> I loved my Barbie dolls. I liked to create stories — soap operas, really — with my dolls...so perhaps that affirms the importance of my role as a storyteller through my weekly coaching newsletter and other content.
>
> — Jill Allison Bryan

> One of my favorite toys was a doll named Tiny Tears. The important metaphor for me now is I shouldn't judge my emotions as they surface in my creative work. It will help me learn how to be supportive to others in their creative explorations.
>
> — Terilee Wunderman

> One of my favorite toys was playing jacks. This toy might represent coordination, rhythm, skill building, and appreciation for design. How I loved the shape of my jacks! The message for me right now is to remember how adept I became with practice and enjoyment, and to not give up.
>
> — Karen Dale

Think of some of your favorite toys as a child, maybe four or five of them. Draw a quick sketch of these toys, make a written list of them, or do an online search for images you can print and make into a collage.

Look over your images or your list, and imagine this is your bag of toys. How might these toys help you as you move into the next steps of your journey? What is the significant message of each?

ACROWHIM
TOY = Tapping Our Youth

HAIKOODLE

play as a toy chest
keeping old friends together
they don't gather dust

TIME TO DOODLE

24 Shimmerviews and Interviews

FUN FACT: Role play — specifically, imitating people of stature or those held in high esteem — is a play behavior that is observed across the world.

If you could spend a day in the shoes of a famous person
— living or dead — whom would you pick?
How might this person handle the project you are manifesting?

One day when Kai was three or so, we were making art and working with a large set of colored pens. I instructed him to carefully pick out one colored pen at a time to work with and then to put it back before getting another one. At one point, Kai tried to pull a pen from the package, and a bunch of purplish pens accidentally fell on the floor. I said, "Oh, all the purples!" and bent down to pick them up. Kai got a very apologetic look on his face, and said, "No, not *on purples* — it was an accident!" Doing something "on purpose" may have worrisome connotations for a toddler, but the truth is that when it comes to our creative dreams, *purpose is everything.*

Finding Your Purpose

Finding your purpose...apparently, everyone is doing it; my Google search yielded over 151 million results on the topic. A purpose is more than a trend, though — you can't just do it because everyone else is. You have to find it for yourself.

Can you easily articulate your life purpose? Perhaps you have a strong sense of what your purpose is but may not feel very confident in trying to explain it to others. Sometimes people get stuck in the Hop phase by thinking things like "I really don't know what I want" or "I know what I want but have no idea how to describe it." Chances are, you *do* know quite a bit about what you want but just need to get in touch with it. Luckily, play can help you have fun as you Hop into identifying and articulating your vision.

Merge play with purpose by imagining that you are being interviewed. In Artella Land, we call my interview series "Shimmerviews" because the purpose (or should I say the *purples*?) of the series is to invite the interview subject to shine. I also love shimmerviewing my clients during classes and coaching sessions; the format seems to have a magic effect on their clarity of vision and the way they express themselves. See the sidebar for an example of a shimmerview.

TRY THIS: RISE AND SHINE

Put yourself in the spotlight and interview yourself from a point in the future when you have manifested your current desires. This is a great tool to play with while you are in the shower or driving in a car by yourself, because you have the privacy to talk out loud. Except, if you are driving, please don't talk with your hands.

You can even try doing this with a friend, where each of you takes turns asking the questions. This allows you to stretch your sense of who you are and where you are, while in the presence of someone else.

Here are a few questions to get you started:

- You've accomplished some really impressive things over the past couple of years! What are you most proud of?
- What do you love most about your life right now?

STORY OF A SHIMMERVIEW

Paula Swenson is a talented coach and artist who works closely with me in the ARTbundance Certification Training program as our ARTbundance associate trainer. Here is how she describes her shimmerview experience:

In early 2010, I participated in the ARTbundance Certification Training program. Near the end of the course, Marney took us on a surprise journey (with no chance to prepare) into the Parallel Universe, two years in the future, where she interviewed each of us about our wild successes.

At the time, I was on the verge of bankruptcy, living in a small Czech town teaching English to adults and trying to find my way back to a creative and abundant life. While some of the things I elaborated on in my interview have not come to pass, I did share my enormous success running live creativity workshops in exotic international locales. Three years later, I ran a workshop on the Greek island where I now live, and so many times during the week, I stood there, watching workshop participants from three continents diving into their creative selves, shaking my head and thinking, "This is real! This is real!" Back in that imaginary time-traveling interview, I envisioned it as an accomplished fact, and in time, it came to be because I had a clear vision to guide my actions. This is very powerful stuff; this is not a silly exercise. This changed my life.

- What are the most fun aspects of your day-to-day life?
- Two years ago, you set a goal for yourself, and now look what has happened. What was the most important thing you did to make it come to pass?
- What advice might you give people who want to achieve what you have achieved?
- What has been *your* secret to playful manifesting?

HAIKOODLE

play as dialogue
hearts shared in conversation
voices holding hands

25   **A List in Wonderland**

FUN FACT: In the Disney animated film *Alice in Wonderland*, the scene from the book where Alice encounters the Jabberwocky was cut, as the beast was thought to be too scary.

What is the scariest part of planning your dream?
What would your Planning Beast look like?

lice in Wonderland is an enchanting adventure because it is full of surprises, puzzles, unexpected changes, and nonsense; it is a world where things aren't what they seem. The more that Alice tries to find order in her new world — solving riddles, doing her multiplication tables, reciting memorized poems — the more she realizes that the order she seeks is not possible. Alice is most successful in Wonderland when she *gives in* to the chaos, surrenders to her "curiouser and curiouser" surroundings, and plays along with the nonsense around her.

A New Look at Lists

In the Hop phase, you will no doubt be making lists at some point, as lists are important to most people when they think of getting things done or planning for next steps. What is your experience with making lists? I enjoy making lists but find myself forgetting to *look* at them. I'd like to be a realist with my lists instead of making my lists unlisted so I can't enlist them.

Seriously, there needs to be *something* that draws me in and reminds me to look. As usual, a playful approach makes all the difference for me. How might you ensure that *your* approach to lists is filled with magic and wonder? How might a list help keep you from falling down the rabbit hole and being overwhelmed, and instead gently usher you into a wonderful world in which you are poised to Skip and Jump?

TRY THIS: PLAYFUL LIST MAKING

Here are some ideas to add a bit of play to your list making:

- What would "Wonderland" mean to you? Is your version of Wonderland full of color or monochromatic? Is it represented by mysterious tunnels or mystical trees? Doodle elements of *your* Wonderland all around your lists. Every time you complete something on the list, you can add something else to the picture. This is how you change your to-do list into a to-*doodle* list!

- Replace your regular to-do list with a big piece of poster board or a large dry-erase board, on which you will write a list with markers. Write with your nondominant hand, or put the marker in your fist with the point perpendicular to the poster board, so you can make really broad, childlike strokes as you write. Use different colors, and let it be fun. How does it feel to write a grown-up list in this childlike way?

ACROWHIM
LIST = Lost Inside Still Time

HAIKOODLE

play as a long list
grown-up things that were not done
fun was had instead

TOP TEN SIGNS YOU ARE OBSESSED WITH LISTS

10. You are feeling overcome by unexplainable bliss right now.
9. You pour out the milk and throw away perfectly good food, just so you can make a shopping list.
8. You avoid taking action, just so your to-do list can get longer and longer every day.
7. Your collection of lists has become a viable alternative to wallpaper.
6. When someone asks, "How are you doing today?" you whip out your notebook and a pen.
5. You make lists about making lists.
4. Your loved ones know to request a list before getting you a gift.
3. You think Santa has the best job ever.
2. You write your personal letters in list format.
1. You are closing this book immediately so you can write at least ten of your own "top ten" lists.

SECTION TWO

SKIP

26 I Skip, You Skip, Everybody Skips

FUN FACT: In 1935, Fred A. Birchmore circled the globe by bicycle, covering forty thousand miles and wearing out seven sets of tires.

If you could take your dream around the world and were not limited by anything but your imagination, how would you travel?

When I first got the contract for this book, I knew one of my first steps would be to interview the coolest Skipper I know. No, it's not Barbie's little sister. It's Kim Corbin, who, in addition to being my publicist at New World Library, founded the worldwide skipping movement in 1999. Her website, iSkip.com, "belongs to all of the skippers of the world" and encourages skipping — literally — as a way to fitness, fun, and freedom.

Lessons from Skipping

I shared with Kim the concept of the Skip phase in the context of Hop, Skip, Jump: Skipping is where we try different things and cover a lot of ground. But we also might tire ourselves out, so we need to stop and start as necessary. Skipping is imperative for gaining momentum and is the place where we build substance to create the kind of sturdy support we need to Jump with conscious intention. Kim resonated with this metaphor and shared with me the great impact that the literal act of skipping can have for adults:

> Skipping gives us an opportunity to play with other people's judgments. It is a great way to exercise our own creative joy and say, "This is fun," worrying less and less about what other people think of you. The positive energy of skipping really takes you back to something that is so familiar and freeing. It brings you back to the beginner's mind, where you can't do anything wrong. It's a great way to blast through fear of any kind. You don't have to plan; you just *skip*.

Moving your body is a great way to move your dream. Movement begets movement. Look at children's natural inclination to create with their bodies: they want to run, jump, play, dance, and catch fireflies, during the early ages before body image and self-consciousness arise, and before sedentary activities become more hypnotic than the natural world. The Skip phase is about *increasing momentum*, and what better way to do that than moving your body?

TRY THIS: DON'T PLAN, JUST SKIP!

When you feel you are in a lull, move your body! But instead of going to the gym, where all those icky stress levels permeate the air, try these alternatives:

- Go to a local playground. Play hopscotch, pump your legs on the swing, or climb jungle gyms.
- Garden, hike, or roll down a hill to connect with nature.
- Visit iSkip.com to get some great ideas about skipping.
- Blow bubbles and chase them. Fly a kite. Attempt a cartwheel. Move like a child. Trust your body to create momentum, even when you *think* you don't have any.

HAIKOODLE

play as little skips
feeling like a child again
legs make the world move

27   **Modular Manifesting**

FUN FACT: The Spirograph toy was dubbed "a new use of the wheel" by its inventor, Denys Fisher.

What does the phrase "reinvent the wheel" mean to you when you think of your own productivity? How might reinventing the wheel feel like fun?

s you transition from the Hop phase to the Skip phase, you move your idea out of your head and into the realm of moving, experimenting, and trying new things. You might stay in this phase for a long time, as if you were skipping around Disneyland on a free weekend pass, in no hurry to see all the sights. Or your time in the Skip phase might just be a quick ride around the block with your bike on training wheels. You could also *skip* Skipping altogether, but I wouldn't recommend it. Your manifestation process would be rather lopsided, and besides, it would be a big waste of paper since Skipping is one-third of this book.

An Alternative to Linear Productivity

In the Skip phase, *action is modular but not linear*. This means:

* Each action you take is important, no matter how big or small.

- Taking *any* action is more important than taking actions in the correct order.

The word *modular* refers to a building concept used in everything from constructing homes to designing computer programs and scientific experiments. A modular process is one that involves separate pieces of a whole coming together in a flexible fashion. In my more playful explorations of the word, I learned that *modular* has only one exact rhyme — *nodular* — and though my rhyming dictionary says there are several near rhymes, none of them pass muster with me. For example, *modular* does *not* rhyme with *jocular*, but I share this fact because I really like the word *jocular*.

You engage in modular manifesting whenever you *follow your energy.* The steps you take *will* build on each other, but not necessarily in a sequential, linear order. Let me be clear: I'm not against doing things in the proper order. If "taking the next logical step" works for you, then by all means, do it — but *not* if following the linear sequence comes at the risk of getting stuck.

I look back at the trajectory of my business over the past dozen years, and there are so many things I would have done differently in the name of efficiency if I had known then what I do now. But that's the point — I *didn't* know it then. Furthermore, if I had waited to learn how to do things in the "proper" order, I probably would have lost all my momentum and given up. With Skip energy, we understand *the productive purpose of taking steps out of order.*

Though much of society still clings to the "work hard, make it happen" approach, the Skip phase lets you create a new system that encourages, rather than alienates, your intuitive instincts. Using Skip energy, you can gracefully pivot away from society's tireless push to Jump and to do it like everyone else. In your new paradigm of action, you can finally understand the great value in Skipping — and in Skipping *your* own way.

TRY THIS: MAKE YOUR LINKIN' LOGS

1. Cut out some log-like shapes from brown paper or card stock, or use your crayons to color them brown.

2. On each log, write an action you know gives you a boost of energy. Here are some prompts to get you started:

   I have a lot of fun when I _____.
   I usually get a boost of energy when I _____.
   A quick way to get me in a good mood is _____.
   I feel jocular* when I _____.

3. Whenever you feel stuck, reach for one of the logs, and do the action written on it. This will help you make the *link* between movement — *any* movement whatsoever — and modular manifesting.

MANIFESTAGRAM
Manifest = "Amen" fits!

HAIKOODLE

play as wood toy logs
fit together notch by notch
building tiny dreams

---

* As stated above, I am deeply tickled by the word *jocular*, but you should feel free to replace it with your own joy-inducing word.

28 The Brilliance of Shiny Objects

FUN FACT: Ring pops — lollipops shaped like jeweled rings that graced many a childhood romance — have made a comeback as a popular way for brides to "propose" to their bridesmaids.

If your dream were to propose to you and ask you to commit to it for better or worse, how would you feel?

Last year, during a beach vacation, Kai's favorite activity was to go "treasure hunting" on the beach with a metal detector. It was so much fun to see his face light up as he found amazing "treasures." He found some coins and bottle caps, and his coup was a toy train. He was, however, disappointed that he didn't find any sparkly jewelry for me, as that was his goal. However, he had a backup plan: to take his metal detector to a *graveyard* because he was sure to find wedding rings under the ground. I have to say, it's a brilliant solution, albeit creepy. Not to mention, you know, illegal.

Objectivius Shinium Syndromus

The phrase "shiny object syndrome" gets a lot of buzz today. It refers to people who invariably get distracted by something shiny and new. Most often, this is a phrase used critically. Entrepreneurs and empowerment coaches often use the phrase synonymously with *procrastination* or "creative ADD." However, the Skip phase helps us see that *this "syndrome" is actually a superpower.*

If you are drawn to "shiny things," stand up and be proud! This is an amazing gift because it means you have a sophisticated inner detection system that works instantly to lead you to your excitement. Remember — what moves us *is* what moves us. The longer you are stuck, the longer you stay stuck. This is why the ability to see and follow shiny objects is so important — shiny objects are portals to play and will get you moving.

Have you ever had several of the lightbulbs in your home burn out at the same time? I've always found this curious, given how electricity use obviously varies from room to room. Nevertheless, the lightbulbs seem to be in cahoots to burn out together, those little rascals. Your internal electric source works the same way. When your creativity fizzles out, it affects *all* areas of your life: general mood, productivity, relationships, focus and attention, quality of rest and sleep…the list goes on and on! On the other hand, when your creative spark is renewed, it magically "turns on" all other areas in your life as well.

TRY THIS: HUNTING FOR TREASURES

Imagine you have a metal detector that goes "beep, beep, beep" when it lands on a shiny object. It is intrinsically woven with your soul. Without any effort from you, it lights up when you light up, and leads you to the play portals you may not have noticed.

Walk through a room and listen for the "beep, beep, beep." What sparkly thing draws you in? Where do your eyes and heart take you?

Go through your day and see where your detector leads. Whenever you get that unmistakable signal — "beep, beep, beep" — that means something shiny is around, and there is reason to dig! Keep a treasure journal to help you remember where you found something shiny. When you're stuck, the sparkle will take you right where you need to go.

If you are looking around and you're not hearing that "beep, beep, beep," try going to some new places outside of your regular routine. Go to new stores, take a new route, visit new websites, read new magazines, strike up conversations with new people. Eventually, something *will* spark. When it does, follow it. Just don't go to a graveyard, please.

ACROWHIM
SHINY = See Here! It's a New "Yes!"

HAIKOODLE

play as a bright jewel
sparkling in the sun and shade
extravagant flash

Feel free to doodle

29 Creative Cartography

FUN FACT: Etch A Sketch was originally called *l'écran magique* (magic screen).

*If your future could flash across a magic screen,
what would you like to see?*

When Kai was four, he had a big temper tantrum. Naturally, I don't even remember what it was about. In the midst of it, he stormed into his playroom, sat down at a table with an orange marker and paper, and began scribbling furiously and intently. As he continued his scribbling fervor, I checked in on him. Here's how our conversation went:

ME: Hey, buddy, what are you drawing?
KAI: A *map*.
ME: Oh? What kind of map?
KAI: A map to *get out of here*.
ME: You mean get out of the playroom?
KAI: No…
ME: You mean out of the house?
KAI: No! To get out of feeling so angry!

I didn't know whether to laugh or cry. Of course, I was sad that he was feeling such intense emotion, but I was delighted that he had figured out how to use his creativity to help him try to deal with his big feelings. I made a scan of the scribbles so I could keep "Map out of Feeling So Angry, circa 2012" forever.

Mapping and Manifesting

As you Skip around trying new things, a map is a useful tool. A map will help you navigate your feelings, your thoughts, and your ideas. For thousands of years, maps have helped us see where we are going. In my art, I love painting on old maps, because it feels like having a dialogue with lines, shapes, colors, and spaces as new images become part of the old geography.

Here's something most people don't know about maps: you can make a map *as you go*. A map doesn't have to be created ahead of time. While you may not want to take this approach when driving to an important appointment, when it comes to manifesting, a map can function as a living document — one that lives, breathes, and changes with you. Think of your map as a daring diary of your adventures rather than a preconceived pathway of your plans.

TRY THIS: YOU ARE HERE

Create a new map to explore your movement in the Skip phase. Try adding something new to the map every day. Simply add a spot on your map to claim, "I skipped here!" Along the way, you can also make marks to record your emotional arc — the ups and downs of your feelings.

The map that graphs your skips and charts your feelings doesn't need to be fancy or "artistic." Try crayon scribbles on a piece of paper or pencil sketches on a paper plate. The most simple, playful map is one that will help you find your way.

HAIKOODLE

play as an old map
GPS for olden times
roads to adventure

30 Improvisational Skipping

FUN FACT: In Calgary in 1977, Keith Johnstone, inspired by street wrestling matches, originated Theatresports, "a competition between teams of improvisers," as a family-oriented, audience-interactive event involving competing improv teams, an emcee, and a panel of judges.

Think of a current frustration or challenge in terms of it being a theatrical sport. How might you improvise your way out of it?

I attended a performing arts high school, where I studied theater and took improv classes. In an earlier career, I taught improv games to educators in inner-city schools. More recently, I introduced some improv games to the kids in our homeschool co-op. Even more recently than *that*, just this morning, I realized that Kai didn't have any clean socks, so I improvised and gave him a pair of mine. See how *versatile* improv is?

Lessons from Improv

Improv — also called "impro" — has been used as an effective team-building tool for a long time, way before our bigwig business consultants came along and started introducing it in conference rooms. In fact, I wouldn't be surprised if America's bigwig forefathers — literally, the men who wore big wigs — did some impro to come together and sign the Declaration of Independence.

One of the golden rules in improvisation games is "Always say yes." If someone on your team pretends to throw something to you, saying, "Here, catch! It's a heavy sword!" you aren't allowed to say, "No it's not — it's a baby bunny!" You also don't say, "What? I don't see anything. There's nothing there! You're just pretending, aren't you?" because, well, that just isn't playing fair.

My client Barbara Krauss has built two coaching and speaking companies, the Centre for Organic YESipes and Y5 Ventures, on the concept of "saying *yes*." In a coaching session with me, she explained her core drive: "Giving yourself the gift of saying *yes* means getting out of your own way, remembering who you really are, touching the possibilities in your life, and unfolding the parts of you that used to make you come alive."

"Saying yes" doesn't mean agreeing to every opportunity that comes your way as you are Skipping about. It *does* mean looking for the yes as often as you can, even when you are actually saying no. For example, if I decline to bake quiche for a party, I'm really saying *yes* to something else — to myself, my family, my other projects, and, especially, the people who may not yet realize that I'm useless in a kitchen and that everyone would be much happier if I just brought the ice.

TRY THIS: YES TICKETS

Here's a fun way to practice saying yes:

1. Cut or tear some paper into small pieces so that you have a pile of blank slips of paper. Aim for twenty or so slips. These will become your "yes tickets."

2. Grab your colorful markers, and on each slip of paper, write one word that represents something you love. The words can be anything — adjectives, verbs, nouns. They can be directly related to what you want to manifest or just words that pop into your mind as you think of things you love. Aim to move quickly; don't stop to think. Change colors every so often so that you have lots of

different colors in your pile. The first words that pop into my mind right now are: *flowers, wisdom, trust, collage, orange, giggles, ocean, clouds, piano, eyes, lucky, snuggles, pink, tender, chenille, Laverne, Shirley, perforated papers.* (I always thought the *Laverne & Shirley* theme song said, "Chenille, schnozzle, hot and pepper perforated.")

3. After your pile is complete, shuffle it all around. Then ask an open-ended question about what you are manifesting. Here are some examples:

   What do I most need to know right now?
   What am I not seeing?
   What would be the most helpful action for me to take?
   What does the theme song from *Laverne & Shirley* really mean?

4. Close your eyes. Pick two tickets, and read the words on them. Imagine that these two words, together, are the secret answer to your question, and say yes!

See the sidebar for an example of this process.

EXAMPLE OF USING YES TICKETS

I asked, "What's the best way I might organize my overstuffed file cabinet?" The answer, according to my yes tickets, was "ocean giggles." If I were to say yes to this answer, what might that mean?

- When I think of an ocean, I think of abundance — lots to see. If I could see my file cabinet as abundant instead of overwhelming, perhaps that would make it more fun and giggly to splash in.
- What if I could work on it in waves rather than just doing it all at once?
- What if I searched for giggles as I organized? What if my sorting criteria were related to giggles — giggle worthy or not giggle worthy?

Ahh... I am already feeling so much more energy flowing toward this task — just from saying *yes!*

HAIKOODLE

play as jazz improv
riffing chords and melodies
making it all up

31 What Butterflies Know about Manifesting

FUN FACT: *The Very Hungry Caterpillar*, the children's book by Eric Carle, has sold the equivalent of one copy per minute since its publication.

What is your life very hungry for right now?

Perhaps there is no better symbol for transformation and manifestation than the butterfly and its process of moving from caterpillar to cocoon to butterfly. Butterflies are often used as a symbol to show the "payoff" of hard work: "Look how hard the caterpillar has to work, and as a result, it becomes a butterfly." Why is being a butterfly any more special than being a caterpillar? Why is an hour of meditating any more sacred than an hour of washing the dishes? Why is five minutes of blowing bubbles with a child more playful than five minutes of organizing your weekly receipts? It doesn't have to be. Play is a state of mind.

Pausing Instead of Pushing

A person who studies butterflies is called a lepidopterologist. I am not a lepidopterologist, primarily because I am not able to pronounce it, but also because I have not studied all things butterfly. So I'm not an expert. Yet I'd like to think that a caterpillar, when building its cocoon, is not necessarily "working hard," but simply following its true nature and taking its time. A playful manifestation process means trusting divine timing. It means that when something seems to be taking a long time, maybe it's not a sign that we need to push harder, but rather a sign that we need to *pause.*

I once visited a butterfly garden and watched as all the children ran around trying to catch butterflies. I found myself walking around looking at the different butterfly species and enjoying the fairy-esque delight. I wasn't chasing the butterflies like the kids, but my inner conversation was saying, "I need to keep moving — I don't want to miss anything!" Then at one point, I got a little tired of walking, and I sat down on the ground and closed my eyes. I felt a small tickle on my right arm. Not one, but two butterflies had landed on my hand like two little glittering cherubs.

In manifesting what you want, *sometimes pausing is more important than pushing.* As you're Skipping, you're not being timed by some kind of divine stopwatch in the sky. You get to take your time. Skipping becomes more sustainable when it also leads you to quiet places, slow breaths, and cocoons of faith.

TRY THIS: MAKE A METAMORPHIC MEMO

1. Draw two large circles, side by side, with their edges barely touching.

2. In the middle of one of circle, write the word "stop." Add decorations, doodles, or other words or phrases that come to mind when you think of taking time to *stop,* pause, and be present.

3. In the middle of the other circle, write the word "watch." Add decorations, doodles, or other words or phrases that come to mind when you think of *watching* the world around you, taking it all in.

4. Draw a vertical line between the two circles, and you'll

see a butterfly emerge. Add more embellishments to make the butterfly come to life.

5. This butterfly is here with a simple reminder: Stop. Watch. You're *not* on the clock. You can take all the time you need. So enjoy a pause and watch for a little gift to alight on your wrist.

MANIFESTAGRAM
Chasing butterflies = A cherub's tinsel gift

HAIKOODLE
play as butterflies
filling a field with color
do-it-yourself wings

Don't forget to doodle

FUN FACT: Apparently, *quizzify* is Scrabble's most valuable eight-letter word: if used in the right place, it's worth 419 points, as only one *z* is available and a blank must be used for the other.

Make a quiz about your life story.
Give it to a few people, and see how well they know you.

I recently was at a hospital for a routine lab appointment and was stuck in the elevator for a short time. It was nothing dramatic — it couldn't have been more than about five minutes — but during the time we were stuck, I had a great time with a handful of strangers. A man says to the woman next to the controls, "Hey, I thought you were driving this thing," and everyone kind of chuckles. Then he says, "Well, is anyone serving drinks?" Another man holds up his chalky medicinal mixture — for CT-scan contrast, I imagine — and says, "I've got a drink!" The chuckles switch to a laugh. Then another person points out someone is carrying a urine collection jug and says, "Hey, I'd rather have that than what *she's* carrying," and suddenly we're all just cracking up. It was a moment of spontaneous bonding with strangers whom I most likely won't see again — although if anyone in the elevator with me on March 28, 2014, is reading this, thank you for showing me that even being stuck in an elevator in a hospital can be playful!

Play Can Make Someone Else's Day

People who naturally gravitate to Skipping often find a meaningful life comes from meaningful connections with others. They are often natural magnets to other people, and as a result, they attract interesting opportunities. Sharing a playful energy in the world is a great way to open conversations, make connections, and expand your opportunities. As you go about your day-to-day life, how might you invite a stranger to play?

The fun in the elevator happened because one person decided to be playful. Because of his choice, I went to my appointment with a smile on my face, and I imagine the others did, too. It seemed like everyone in my path was nicer than usual. The phlebotomist told me I had a great smile. A woman in the waiting room commented on my shoes, and we talked about our love for bright colors. The valet told me to "have a blessed day," and I looked him in the eye and said, "Thank you. I am."

Studies have shown that, interestingly, positive interactions with *strangers* make a greater difference in our mood than positive interactions with those close to us. The results of these studies encouraged people to give passersby a nod, greeting, or other acknowledgment. While you're at it, why not share a bit of play, levity, whimsy, silliness, or the kind of smile that comes from your eyes as well as your lips. That good-humored man in the elevator set a playful tone for the rest of my day. To whose day will *you* bring play?

TRY THIS: COLLECTING SMILES

This exercise works best if you are wearing something with two pockets. If you don't have pockets, I invite you to playfully improvise another solution, such as collecting your smiles with a pen and a small notebook. If you *do* have pockets, here are the steps:

1. Grab a handful of coins and put them in one pocket. This is great way to use the spare change hiding in the backs of desk drawers or under floor mats in the car.
2. Each time you share eye contact and a smile with someone, move a coin from one pocket to the other.
3. At the end of the day, gather all the coins you moved from one pocket to the other and put them into a jar or container. If you're running short on spare change, you can simply count up the number of coins and keep a written log of how much you "earned" during the day.
4. Repeat this the next day. Try it for at least a full week. At the end of the week, you can use the "smile savings" you've collected to buy a fun new toy.

This exercise will make you aware of how often you smile, and as a result, you'll start looking for more smiles to exchange. You'll see how you can use Skip energy to move from person to person with authentic connections. You'll also feel yourself getting richer — the more you give, the more you get!

ACROWHIM

OTHERS = Oh! These Humans Empathize
Rather Sincerely

HAIKOODLE

play as shared laughter
starts as a giggle, then boom!
rhythm beyond blues

33 Make Your OH!dometer

FUN FACT: Video arcade racing games, which first became popular in the late 1970s, have inspired a variety of subgenres, including futuristic racing games that feature science fiction settings, abstract vehicles, and defiance of the laws of physics.

If you could create an imaginary vehicle that would help you manifest your dream more quickly and easily, what features, goodies, and gadgets would it include?

What one word best describes how you most want to feel every day? The word could be anything — examples might include *joyful*, *peaceful*, *excited*, *present*, *alive*, *aware*, and *connected*. While there might be many words that could describe how you'd like to feel — you might look at my sample list and say, "Yeah, all of the above, please" — see if you can whittle it down to just *one* word. My word is *playful*. If I am feeling playful, everything else seems to fall into place.

Your Ultimate Motivator

Your one word represents your *OH!*, which is an acronym for "one hunger!" It is the thing you want more than anything else, the core of who you are. It is your ultimate motivator (the acronym for which happens to be *YUM*). Knowing your OH! is a wonderful way to know yourself.

During the Skip phase, it's really important to keep a gauge on your energy level, commitment, and motivation. Just as in actual physical skipping, it is this phase where you are at risk for getting tired because you are using a lot of energy. Your energy is replenished when you are fulfilling your OH!, when your one hunger is being fed. When your OH! is slipping, it means your momentum, motivation, and commitment are slipping as well. By keeping track of your OH!, you learn when you feel most like *you* and when you don't. Your OH! teaches you to nourish yourself. Much like *om*, the Sanskrit mantra you may have chanted in meditation or yoga class, your OH! is something you can repeat whenever you need to bring your focus back to yourself. You also might try saying, "Yum, OH!, and om, oh my!" ten times fast and see if you can keep yourself from laughing.

TRY THIS: YOUR DAILY OH! READING

Use your OH! word to create an "OH!dometer." Your OH!dometer is a playful tool that invites you to check in to get a reading on your OH! at any time. You might create a number scale (for example, rating how much you are experiencing your OH! on a scale from one to ten) or even create a rating system using something other than numbers, like colors or flowers. Once you have figured out a system that feels easy and playful, create a physical object that invites you to rate your OH! frequently. For example, you might draw a symbol of your OH!dometer on poster board, reinvent a board game spinner, or decorate a pocket-size sketchbook with a representation of your OH!dometer and take the sketchbook with you on the road.

Regardless of the physical form you create, if you place your OH!dometer somewhere where you will see it often, you will be reminded to take an OH!dometer reading often. When it's reading low, you can intervene with an activity to boost it. This is a great way to make sure you're keeping tabs on your own energy as you're Skipping along.

HAIKOODLE

play as one hunger
waiting to be fed and filled
feast upon your life

TOP TEN SIGNS YOU WORK TOO MUCH

10. You wonder where the day went — at 9:00 AM.
9. Your to-do list is bigger than your address book.
8. The last five books you read had either the word *time*, *stress*, or *deadline* in the title.
7. Well, okay, they were really *audio*books, but you've got to do something during your commute.
6. The only movies you've seen this year were on airplanes.
5. The last time you didn't work during a meal was Thanksgiving.
4. Prison inmates get more conjugal visits with their spouses than you do.
3. For her third birthday, you bought your daughter her very own day planner.
2. You now wear a wireless headset all day to disguise the fact that you talk to yourself constantly.
1. Even those "free vacation" telemarketers have put you on their do-not-call list.

The Sparkle
Scavenger Hunt

FUN FACT: Geocaching (www.geocaching.com) is a real-world treasure hunt in which over six million participants worldwide hide and
retrieve containers in the out-of-doors.

*If you could go on a treasure hunt to find exactly what you need
for your dream right now, what would be on your list?*

When Kai was in preschool, his teacher used a behavior-
tracking system where the kids had little colored cubes
and followed a color scale of behavior. The kids would
move up and down the color scale throughout the day, according
to their choices. Positive choices meant they could move up to
the next color on the scale; unfortunate choices meant they had
to move down a color. Frankly, it seemed rather complicated, and
I wondered how in the world the teacher was able to track the
cube colors of a whole room full of four-year-olds. I wonder if
she had nightmares about cubes, or colors, like Tippi Hedren's
character in the movie *Marnie*, who freaks out whenever she
sees the color red. I love that movie because a young, very hot
Sean Connery keeps saying my name. I'd love *that* on a video
loop.

But I digress. In Kai's preschool class, the cube that represented the very highest level was called the "sparkle cube." In our

house, we set up big rewards for the "sparkle" days — they didn't happen too often — and I found myself wishing I could have sparkle days myself. So I started my sparkle list, which became an ongoing scavenger hunt for self-care.

Skipping in Self-Care

Like the Hop and Jump phases, the Skip phase has its potential risks. People who are naturally inclined to Skip don't even realize how *tired* they can become in all their frolicsome movement. Caroline described it beautifully: "I do so much, and since I enjoy it all, I don't realize the toll it's taking on my body. When I get sick or have a health issue, it takes me by surprise because I *think* I'm just enjoying it all. But I can't do everything, even if everything is inspiring."

Ironically, when you are doing things you really enjoy, it's harder to *stop* moving than it is to start moving. We need playful systems to Skip in self-care.

I tell my entrepreneurial clients, "Taking care of yourself *is* taking care of your business." We all need to remember to go back to basics and get a strong hold on what we really need each day to take care of ourselves. I find it's so much easier to maintain a self-care system when it feels playful.

What Is a "Really Good Day"?

What does a "really good day" look like to you?

For my sparkle list, I started by making a list of what happens in a really good day. My sparkle list has changed over time in both format and content. In terms of format, I started by using a simple list that I wrote out each week on a dry-erase board. Then I began writing it in my day planner so I could keep a week-to-week record. For a while, I used a spreadsheet that I printed out weekly. These days, I'm using a list app on my phone.

The content of the list has changed, too. My first sparkle list consisted of entirely *doable* things, but over time, I've pushed myself to stretch it a bit. When I first started this practice, my list simply consisted of random actions; now I organize my list according to five types of health:

- *Physical health* — things I want to do every day for my physical health
- *Mental health* — things I want to do every day to maintain my mental clarity
- *Emotional health* — things I want to do each day to ensure my emotional needs are met
- *Systemic health* — things I want to do each day to take care of the organization of systems and structures, such as the organization of living areas or the maintenance of electronic systems
- *Mystical health* — things I want to do each day to touch something bigger than me

TRY THIS: A SPARKLE LIST FOR YOUR SPARKLIEST SELF

Here are instructions for making your own sparkle list:

1. Start small. Write down *one* thing you want to be sure to do every day, in order to ensure health and well-being in each of the five categories listed below. Keep it simple, and name actions you *know* you can do. For example:

   Physical health — brush my teeth
   Mental health — turn on my web blocker at least once during the day to help me focus
   Emotional health — journal for five minutes
   Systemic health — put the mail where it goes instead of just throwing it somewhere
   Mystical health — appreciate one thing of beauty during the day

2. Make some kind of checklist so you can check the items off as you do them.

3. Resist the urge to add anything new to your sparkle list until you go through several days of getting 100 percent sparkle. Hitting 100 percent every day feels great and builds confidence. Once you've gotten 100 percent consistently, you can slowly start adding more things to your list. You're one sparkly self-care rock star!

ACROWHIM
SPARKLE = Self-Preservation:
A Radically Kind, Loving Ethos

HAIKOODLE

play as treasure hunt
a list holds the things to find
a heart holds what's found

35 Playing Hide-and-Seek with Beauty

FUN FACT: The largest game of hide-and-seek took place at Stenden University in Qatar in 2012 and involved 1,240 participants.

When you think of what you are manifesting, what might "Ready or not, here I come!" mean?

As you Skip around trying new things, you might be discouraged when your experiments don't turn out as planned. When you can look at these experiences with a playful eye, you might see something that wasn't there on first glance. You might even see beauty. One of the most profound creative experiences I've ever had was when I attended an art conference in 2001 and created a mixed-media assemblage in a class taught by artist Pamela Hastings. I had a wonderful time creating an over-the-top assemblage of a plump woman. But back at the hotel room, I was shocked to see that she looked like a geometric mess that a toddler made. I was tempted to throw her away. I am so glad I didn't, because she changed the path of my life forever.

Hidden Beauty

After the retreat, I could feel her continuing to haunt me from a shelf in my studio. I decided I needed to figure out *why* I was so intensely triggered by this piece of art. I needed to play with her and see what she could tell me.

One of my favorite play portals being poetry, I sat down and wrote a free-form poem. Her story was written through me quickly, without thinking, and I was surprised to find out that *she was me*. All the mismatched "stuff" on her represented the collection of tangled, wiry, precious things I had picked out and carried for my journey in life. In this new perspective, she was suddenly the most beautiful thing I had ever seen. It was then that I learned *the uglier we think something is, the more potential it has for beauty*.

This experience led me right into starting *Artella* magazine, which then turned into the company which has been my full-time work for a dozen years. I could never have imagined that looking somewhere unexpected — in this case, an "ugly" piece of art and a story that came from deep within — would lead me onto this new path. Beauty was hiding in that piece of art. I'm so glad I found it.

TRY THIS: READY OR NOT, HERE I COME!

1. Intentionally start with something "ugly." Take something that you've done that you really hate. Or make something despicable right now — maybe you can snap a photo of your totally messy kitchen or something else nearby that you really think is ugly.

2. Close your eyes, count to ten, and then shout out, "Ready or not, here I come!"

3. Open your eyes, and look at whatever is in front of you.

Look with curious eyes, as if you are looking at shapes in the clouds. Look only for beauty.

4. Take a nap. Because, well, it just helps.

MANIFESTAGRAM
Finding the beauty = I hug fate: tiny bend.

HAIKOODLE

play as hide-and-seek
count to ten before you look
peek from squinted eyes

36   Most Valuable
Players

FUN FACT: Artwiculate is a Twitter-based word-of-the-day game for learning new words.

What is one new word you would like to add to your vocabulary that represents the way you think and talk about your dream?

ai invented a game called "Most Valuable of the Day." It goes like this:

1. Walk around mommy's studio and gather interesting things in a bucket: buttons, sequins, old keys, tags, hair barrettes, whatever you can find.
2. Take them to the playroom and pull out the ones that seem valuable. Put the others away.
3. Engage the remaining items in a competition. Place two items head to head, and determine which one is most valuable. Continue through the rest of the pile, until you are left with half.
4. Continue the process to progress to the third, second, and eventually the semifinal and final round. Eventually, you will be left with one item — the most valuable of the day.

Kai is an only child, and is homeschooled, so he is pretty adept at playing games by himself, and this is one of his favorites.

He will often present the winner, followed by a savvy pitch that invites me to visit MostValuableOfTheDay.com. As of this moment, this website does not exist, so dear readers, I invite you to skip on over to reserve the domain!

Finding Your Focus

When you are in the Skipping phase, sometimes it's hard to know *who* the heck you are and what in the world you are doing. If you are a natural Skipper, you will probably be very familiar with the condition called "extreme identity crisis on steroids." Your personal bio might read something like: "I am a silent-movie buff, medical transcriptionist, armchair traveler, wannabe wood carver, unconventional party planner, amateur horticulturalist, retired tap dancer, knowledgeable home plumber, gluten-free baker, and a babysitter in high demand among my nieces and nephews." If you're nodding your head, then yeah, you know what it means to Skip.

On the other hand, if you are *not* usually inclined to do a lot of Skipping, it might feel foreign and uncomfortable to find yourself pulled in so many directions. In either case, a question inevitably comes up: Where should I put my focus? Or, put another way: What is the most *valuable* way I can use my time and energy? With Kai's game, it's actually *fun* to figure out your focus, and it can even change every day, as you learn the skill of tuning in and trusting your instincts.

> ### TRY THIS: PLAY MOST VALUABLE OF THE DAY

1. Write a list of the things you've been doing lately and the topics that have been on your mind. Put each item in the list in the following format, as if you were writing an interesting bio for yourself: "I am a(n) _____."

2. Play Most Valuable of the Day: Take the first two roles in your list and decide which of these roles you value most right now. Note that this could change from day to day or moment to moment, so the goal is not to land on the *only* choice, but to practice the skill of quickly checking in with your own intuition and following it. You can't play this game wrong! Continue with the next two roles, then the next two, and so on, until you've gone through all the items on your list. For each pair, note the "winner."

3. Put all the winners into a "runoff" against one another: Compare the first two winners and decide which is more important to you right now, and note the winner of this round. Continue putting the winners head to head until you have gone through the whole list and are left with one "most valuable of the day" and a runner-up or two.

ACROWHIM
VALUE = Vitality Appraisal Levitates Unique Excellence

HAIKOODLE

play as all my skills
the whole greater than the sum
assembly required

37   Story Circles of Life

FUN FACT: Bingo (sometimes called lotto or beano) is one of the most popular games that is easily played simultaneously by a large group of people.

Imagine you are in a bingo hall filled with people and can yell out any one word when you win. Typically, that word would be "Bingo!" but if you could pick any word to celebrate the kind of life you want to live, what would the word be, and why?

I am a volunteer teacher in our homeschool co-op, and for one of my classes, I had planned a creative curriculum about ways for young children to approach making stories. For the first few weeks, I brought a topic or a prompt to each class, until I realized that I didn't need them. These little kids — ranging from age four to six — were so centered in their imaginations that they didn't need a reason to write a story. They just needed paper and markers. They didn't want to learn about story structure. They wanted their stories to skip around and make no sense. It was clear that they knew much more than I did and that I really needed to be taking a class from them.

Whose Life Story Is This, Anyway?

When kids tell stories, they can skip around, not make sense, be incongruent, and it doesn't matter at all. They embody the Skip energy in their stories. I think we need more of this ourselves as we tell our own life stories and live the stories that we tell about ourselves.

Embodying and enjoying Skip energy means you get to explore all the facets of yourself and allow yourself to do more of what you want, more of the time. Your life becomes less about someone else's story and more about who you really are.

While in the Skip phase, you have the time and leisure to look at the story your life tells about you. How much of your life's storytelling is really true to you, and how much of it is based on the expectations of others? I often work with clients who are stuck in their dreams, and it is only when we look deeper that we realize it's not my client's dream — it's a dream that came from another person, time, or place.

TRY THIS: A TALE OF TWO STORIES

1. Use your crayons to draw a character named Oughta Biography. This is a little persona that represents the story you feel you "oughta" live. Draw or doodle Oughta Biography's body shape, facial expression, clothing, and accessories.

2. Write a short story about this character. Keep the story linear and structured, beginning, "Once upon a time, there was..."

3. Draw a character named Arto Biography. This little rascal represents the life story you were born to live — your life as a work of art. Again, draw or doodle the details of what this character looks like.

4. Write a story about this character. Keep it loose, nonsensical, meandering. Begin with the words "Boom! Pop! Wow! Guess what happened today? It was..."

5. What do you notice about these two sets of drawings and stories? What do they tell you about the story of your life?

> ACROWHIM
> New autobiography = We pay author... Bingo!

HAIKOODLE
play as a story
who knows where it might take you?
once upon a time

38 Manifesting Mood Rings

FUN FACT: The "stone" in a mood ring is really a hollow quartz or glass shell containing thermotropic liquid crystals that temporarily change color when there are changes in body temperature.

*If you had to describe your most playful mood as a color,
what color would you choose, and why?*

I'm sure you've noticed that when you have a particular image, topic, or concept in your mind, you start noticing it everywhere. When I was pregnant, Tony said to me, "Are there really always this many pregnant women walking around?" Obviously, pregnancy was on his mind more than it had ever been before. Whatever we are thinking about, we see more of. Whatever we are feeling, we experience more of. This is the basis of the law of attraction, which is the spiritual law that says like attracts like. The "law of attraction" might also describe what happens when I look at Hugh Jackman, but that's another story.

Follow Your Mood

During the Skip phase, pay attention to your mood. Your mood is what leads you to the invaluable momentum that can be created. I've heard clients ask, "How do I know if I'm following my energy?

How do I know if I'm picking the right thing?" The answer is really simple: *if it feels good, you're following your momentum.* It's that simple.

The trouble is, we're not used to living that way. We think that being productive is supposed to feel *hard.* Some people think, "Okay, this is really hard, so I must be doing something right." In some ways, that is true; when you come up against something difficult, it can be a sign that you are getting closer to breaking through another level of fear. However, you can't just stay there, in a frustrated, confused, and deflated mood. You risk becoming inert. In scientific terms, inertia will do anything it can to stay inert. Inertia is the Grumpy Cat in the world of scientific laws and that pessimistic person who never, ever wants to get in a good mood.

At any given time, your mood is the very best indicator of how you are doing. Your mood is important because it is what will bring you back to momentum. You need to change your mood to find your momentum again. When you're feeling resistance, it's not just some random accident. When there is resistance in the Skip phase, it means that your best choice is to Skip somewhere else to pick up that energy again. Mastering playful manifestation means following your good moods like yummy breadcrumbs through the forest of life.

TRY THIS: MOOD DOODLES

Take a crayon and doodle your mood right now. There is no right or wrong way to do this; simply draw, scribble, or make some marks that illustrate your mood right now.

See how easy that was? It only took a few seconds, right? So now, commit to doing this *three times a day* for the next week. Set an alarm to remind you to do it, to just stop and doodle your mood.

Doodling your mood brings your awareness to how you are feeling at any moment. It also gives you a very helpful log of your mood over time. Look back at your doodles at the end of the week and notice your best and worst moods. Explore the result of good moods and the ways that they help. Learn to trust that a good mood is bringing you right where you need to be — right back into the cozy arms of momentum!

ACROWHIM
DOODLE = Days Offer Opportunities
to Doodle Little Emotions

HAIKOODLE

play as a doodle
squint and it looks like something
cloudgaze with a pen

TIME TO DOODLE

FUN FACT: For the movie *WALL-E*, iPod designer Jonathan Ive was consulted for the design of EVE, who is the love interest of the title character. Her eyes are modeled on Lite-Brite pegs.

When were the last three times your eyes lit up?

I am quite certain I am on close watch by the U.S. government. Kai calls my mother "Bama"; it was the first thing he ever called her as a baby, and it stuck. This is all well and good, except that "Bama" autocorrects as "Obama" in every single electronic device I own. My texts are full of messages like: "Going shopping with Obama" and "We'll come over after I take care of Obama's computer." I'm sure that someone is thinking there is a crazy woman in Texas who is quite delusional about the goings-on in her calendar!

Break the Law and Find the Love

There is one law that I would like to break, though it has nothing to do with the government. It's the law of attraction, which, as I mentioned in the previous chapter, is the concept that reminds us our life experience is a direct reflection of our thoughts and feelings. The law of attraction became popular with the release of the documentary *The Secret* in 2006, though evidence of this philosophy goes back at least as far as the early 1900s.

I don't have a problem with the idea, but I bristle a bit at both its label and its emphasis. For starters, I'm much more likely to believe in something that sounds a little more fun than a "law."

I also think that focusing on what you want automatically puts a subconscious focus on what is lacking rather than what is here, available, and plentiful. On the other hand, focusing on what you *love* automatically adds gratitude and awe into the equation, helping you see what you already have instead of what you are lacking. Try a new approach: apply the *awe* of attraction, which means to focus on what you love rather than focusing on what you want.

Practicing the awe of attraction is easy. There are four simple steps, whose first letters conveniently spell *LOVE*:

1. *Listen.* As you are Skipping around, listen for when you say, "I love …!" — for example, "I love this pen!"

2. *Open.* Open your understanding of what you love and *why* you love it. Get specific — for example, "I love this pen! It seems to just glide along with so little effort!"

3. *Visualize.* Connect to a vision of what you want — for example, "Yes, I want more of *this* — this smooth gliding — in my life."

4. *Explore.* Explore where and when you are brought exactly what you ask for — for example, when do you experience the sensation of gliding along with little effort? Look for it, listen for it, and *love* it!

TRY THIS: MAKE A KA-LOVE-OSCOPE

1. Draw a big circle on a piece of paper, then divide it into four quadrants.

2. Write each of the four LOVE cues — *listen*, *open*, *visualize*, and *explore* — in a quadrant, as shown in the diagram.

3. This is your ka-love-oscope. Just like a kaleidoscope, this simple tool invites you to focus on a single object as the

image magically expands into a dazzling infinity of patterns and colors. When you notice what you love, your capacity to receive suddenly expands in infinite ways. Use your ka-love-oscope to view any moment through the lens of love. See the diagram for an example.

To download a printable template, go to:
www.ArtellaLand .com/hsj-down loads.html

MANIFESTAGRAM
Attraction = Act into art.

HAIKOODLE

play as attraction
drawing to you what you want
a game of magnets

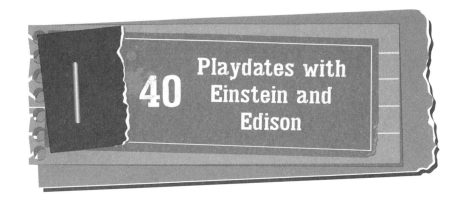

FUN FACT: Silly Putty, which is known for being both a liquid and a solid simultaneously, was taken into space aboard the *Apollo 8* in 1968. It was used as a stress reliever as well as to help fasten things to surfaces.

How would you complete this phrase about yourself?:
I know myself to be both _____ and _____ simultaneously.

I have an Einstein bobblehead, and I just love him. He just sits there and bobs his head up and down, nodding yes to everything I say. Apparently, he thinks I'm brilliant. He's not too shabby himself. Edison is pretty cool, too. It is said that Edison tried something like ten thousand ways to perfect the lightbulb. When asked how he was able to persist after one of his failures, Edison clarified that he did not fail, but simply discovered another way not to improve the lightbulb.

The Sighentific Method

There is an undeniable connection between play and science. Scientific discoveries have been made based on important aspects of play: imagination, invention, spontaneity, and improvisation. In the Skip phase, you can actually use science to do energetic experiments to separate the different particles that are flying around. When you're Skipping through lots of different activities and projects, they can start to meld together and lose their individuality, so science can help you study the individuation of each particular activity.

I'm happy to introduce the *sigh*entific method — the playful process of studying the things that make you sigh, breathe, relax, and have fun. Like the original scientific method, it includes four steps — question, hypothesis, testing, analysis — but it is a lot more fun!

TRY THIS: A PLAYFUL SCIENCE FAIR

1. It's time to get ready for the science fair to examine one or more of your current Skipping interests. Pick one to start — an activity, interest, concept, or idea that is capturing your attention right now.

2. Get some poster board and fat markers to make your science fair display (a regular piece of paper will also work, though it's slightly less playful). Draw or doodle a border around the page with fair-themed images: roller coasters, carousels, cotton candy, the midway. Feel the fun fair energy as you play with this border.

3. In the middle of the page, delineate your sighentific method:

   Question — a question about one of your current Skipping interests
   Hypothesis — what you want to look for in this experiment
   Testing — what you've noticed about your experiences with this particular interest
   Analysis — what this awareness shows you

As you write, decorate your science fair display with fun symbols and doodles of fairgrounds, and allow those fun fair-themed doodles to inspire you. Continue to decorate your display until smiling is inevitable.

See below for an example of using the sighentific method.

SAMPLE SIGHENTIFIC METHOD

1. *Question*: What do I need to know about my interest in handmade paper?
2. *Hypothesis*: There is something here I need to look at.
3. *Testing*: I really like making it. I especially like getting my hands wet and just feeling messy. I like the results but then don't really want to do anything with the paper I make. I feel like I have to make something, though, because of the effort. I wish I had something else to do with it.
4. *Analysis*: I want to look for someone who can use my handmade paper. Perhaps I could trade handmade paper for some help around the house.

ACROWHIM

SCIENCE = Seeing Consciousness In Ever-Nuanced, Changing Evolution

HAIKOODLE

play as a science
life is the experiment
hypothesis: yes

TOP TEN SIGNS YOU'RE A GEEK AT HEART

10. You've named at least one pet after a scientist.
 9. You'd trade food and water for the Discovery Channel.
 8. You wear a lab coat as pajamas.
 7. You think of cooking as an edible science experiment.
 6. You know how much random-access memory (RAM) your computer has.
 5. You've figured out an equation for how much RAM *you* have.
 4. You know the probability of an asteroid hitting the earth.
 3. You have several theories on how to stop this asteroid.
 2. After a sci-fi movie, you'll argue about the physics involved.
 1. You've referred to one million years as "a very short time."

41   Work du Soleil

FUN FACT: Guy Laliberté named his troupe of acrobats Cirque du Soleil (literally translated, "Circus of the Sun") while watching a sunset in Hawaii.

*How might sunrises and sunsets
help you experience more play in your life?*

"My life feels like three-ring circus." When I hear those words, I feel like saying, "Cool, thanks for inviting me! Where are the peanuts?" After all, what could be grander than a life as a circus, to get us out of the drudgery and quiet burnout of the soul. One of my favorite poems is "Damn everything but the circus!" by E.E. Cummings, the text of which hangs in clear view in my office, right next to a hanging acrobat doll I purchased at a Cirque du Soleil gift shop. Whenever I feel too serious during the workday, I read the poem and then give the audacious acrobat a little twirl and watch it spin like a floppy whirligig. The subtle breeze of the doll's movement feels as if a magical trapeze of possibilities is brushing right by me, so close that I can effortlessly and gently grab onto it and take flight.

Imagine a World Where Work Feels Like Play

Look, I get it. Just because the circus can be fun to see, doesn't mean you'd want to *live* there. I personally wouldn't do it because of the smell. But if anyone can somehow arrange a circus that is kind and respectful to animals while smelling like an ayurvedic spa, I'm there.

When you feel like you're looking in many directions, it may be helpful to remember that the initial impetus of the three-ring circus was an expression of *abundance*. Deborah Walk, curator of collections for the Ringling Museums, explains the importance of P. T. Barnum's three-ring setup by saying, "Space wasn't a problem, so why not use it? Philosophically, the explosion of the American circus, the bigness of it all, is the American gift to the circus. Barnum's philosophy was, 'why send out a minnow when a whale will do?'" By learning to embrace the three-ring-circus aspects of the Skip stage, you can *appreciate* the abundance of motion and movement instead of being overwhelmed by it.

An artist recently told me that she was afraid to try to make money from her creations because she didn't want to end up hating them. Her point certainly strikes a chord; we're conditioned to think that if we "work," we'll lose our passion. But it doesn't have to be that way.

For the past few years, I have presented a series of online classes for entrepreneurs called "Work du Soleil," obviously a play on the words *Cirque du Soleil*. The Cirque du Soleil is the consummate example of reinvention: it reinvented the circus to mean high design, beauty, mystery, magic, and a sophisticated twist on whimsy. Circuses have always been magical, but Cirque du Soleil changed magical to *majestic*, and in doing so, became one of the most successful brands in modern years.

The mission of my Work du Soleil series offers this invitation:

What if "hard work"
Could be "work du soleil"?
Just imagine a world
Where work feels like play!

TRY THIS: PLAYING WITH RINGS

1. Write a list of words that describe your very favorite states of being: *joyful, silly, outrageous, daring, colorful, whimsical, bold, fantastical, meaningful, alive…*

2. Pick one word that feels important. Draw a circle on a piece of paper, and in the circle write, "What if work could be _____?" (filling in the blank with your chosen word).

3. Pick another word that feels important. Draw a second circle, and in the circle write, "What if work could be _____?" (filling in the blank with your chosen word).

4. Pick a third word that also feels important. Draw a third circle, and in the circle write, "What if work could be _____?" (filling in the blank with your chosen word).

5. Draw or doodle a picture in each circle to represent your image of work feeling the way you most want to be. As you draw, consider how it feels to allow work — and life — to be all these things. Can you feel the abundance of having three rings in which to play?

MANIFESTAGRAM
Work du Soleil = Soul-like word

HAIKOODLE

play as the circus
the troupe travels town to town
leaves sequins behind

42   Playful Procrastination

FUN FACT: Regardless of what many may think, fortune cookies are distinctly American in origin. In 1992, fortune cookies were imported into Hong Kong and sold as "genuine American fortune cookies."

Imagine you open a fortune cookie to find the ideal fortune that begins, "You will…" What does it say?

When my friend Jean E. threw me a party for my fortieth birthday, a huge bowl containing forty fortune cookies served as the table centerpiece. I would never have imagined that forty fortune cookies would take up so much space! I hadn't had any anxiety about the big birthday, but seeing that bowl actually was a bit of a shock — wow, that is a *lot* of years. I took the cookies home with me, and read one fortune as a playful surprise every day for forty days. If Noah and his animal companions would have had the playful opportunity to read a fun fortune every day, I imagine it would have helped them greatly during their forty days of unfortunate weather.

Is Skipping Procrastination?

One of the fortunate things about Skipping is that what looks like procrastination is actually acceptable, and even welcome. One of the obvious questions about the Skipping phase is "Isn't Skipping just procrastination?" On one level, this is true. You might pivot from one thing to another when you are procrastinating. However, when you are truly procrastinating, your detours look very different than when you are Skipping. When you procrastinate, the detours often include escapist or mind-numbing behaviors (watching bad TV, eating potato chips) or fits of self-flagellation ("What in the world is wrong with me?").

Skipping allows you to make a different choice: *to move toward something that feels good.* Skipping means following your energy to something that is beckoning you. Embracing Skipping feels good; giving in to procrastination doesn't. Skipping is beauty, procrastination is a beast.

Remember: What moves us is what moves us.

Marva Collins-Bush teaches an antiprocrastination workshop called "Anti-Procrastination with Pro-Found Methods." I will proudly declare that I am pro-found. Being pro-found means that I stand for all things that lead me to the truth of life: the profound and playful, the silly and sacred.

TRY THIS:
FINDING PROCRASTINATION'S GOOD FORTUNE

Cut slips of paper, and on each slip, write a simple, playful act. Think in terms of things you could do in five minutes or less. Examples might include:

- Watching a favorite video online
- Dancing to a song
- Drawing a bouquet of flowers with crayons, cutting it out, and putting it in a vase
- Pretending to play hopscotch on the sidewalk
- Singing a song out loud
- Skipping!

Treat these slips of paper like little fortunes inside the cookies of day-to-day life. Whenever you feel the urge to procrastinate, instead of going to one of your less-than-savory behaviors, pick a fortune instead.

ACROWHIM

PROFOUND = Procrastination Readily Offers Fabulous Opportunities to Understand New Directions

HAIKOODLE

play as a cookie
enjoyed as a tasty treat
small hands, many crumbs

43 **Sacred Play**

FUN FACT: The Unemployed Philosophers Guild (www.philosophers guild.com) sells novelty gifts and toys depicting cultural giants in a humorous and often irreverent light. Products include Freudian Slippers, finger puppets of philosophers, and a paper-doll set called Einstein's Ensembles.

Imagine there was a paper doll of yourself
that came with five different outfits, including accessories,
to represent the five most important roles
you've played in your life. What would be included?

As you're happily Skipping along, you will surely encounter challenges: both everyday frustrations and challenges that shake you to your very core. These challenges threaten to stop you mid-Skip and bring your momentum to a halt. Think how often you have heard someone — perhaps even yourself — say, "Everything was going great until *xyz* happened, and then nothing else happened for years." Now, I know that *xyz* must feel downright apocalyptic — why else would it be at the end of the alphabet? But you *can* use play, even in the midst of alphabetic tragedy.

The Cosmic Café

Fourteenth-century Christian mystic Henry Suso is thought to be the first to use the term *ludus amoris*, which is Latin for "game of love" — a term that describes divine play and that has continued to be used in mystical traditions. A tradition I find particularly playful — and extremely helpful during challenging times — is the Hindu interpretation of sacred play.

The Sanskrit word *lila*, like many Sanskrit words, cannot be literally translated to English but can be loosely translated as "play." It refers to the Hindu tradition wherein all reality is seen as play and our lives are thought to be the outcome of creative play by the Divine.

It is this concept that inspires one of the most playful ways to get through a challenging time: *imagine that you are an actor on a cosmic stage, given a role to perform.*

Picture yourself as a bundle of cosmic energy, happily relaxing in a cozy coffeehouse in deep space, sipping your beverage, looking down at what is happening on earth below. You then see that there is an opening for *star* actors (that's you!) to fill the role of a particular person: to *be* that person, with many difficult circumstances, and see what you can make out of them. You rise from your chair, enter the role without the emotional drains that so often accompany personal drama: no guilt, shame, pressure, or expectation. You simply put on your costume and enter stage right.

It is said that when we make plans, God laughs. When you embrace sacred play, *you* get to laugh, too. During one of the most difficult challenges of my life, this playful method saved me and provided the perspective I needed to rise each day and decide to take on the role of playing me, intrinsically connected to the much bigger cosmic café of life.

TRY THIS: CASTING YOURSELF

Write an audition notice for the role of *your* life in this sacred play. You can use the following as prompts:

Seeking _____ to play the role of
_____.
Brief descriptions of the role and its story arc are:
_____.
Special skills required include _____.
Come to the audition ready to demonstrate your best
ability to _____.

HAIKOODLE

play as theater
wearing costumes for our roles
spotlight on the fun

Feel free to doodle

44

Quantum Particles at Play

FUN FACT: Rubik's Cube, with its 43 quintillion possible configurations, has been the subject of many serious scientific papers, such as a study by theoretical physicists at MIT who compared the twists of the cube to states of particles.

How would you be most likely to try to solve Rubik's Cube? Would you consult a written guide? Ask someone else who has mastered it? Obsessively figure it out on your own? How does your response compare to the way you approach your own life and its seemingly infinite number of colorful possibilities?

ecently, Kai came hopping over to me, saying, "Mommy, something is wrong with my foot!" I asked him to show me where, and he said, "Everywhere! It's like little particles — they are buzzing everywhere! What's happening?" I finally figured out it was the first time he had experienced the sensation of his foot being asleep! I explained and we both laughed. Then he said, "It hurts a little and feels a little good when all the particles move around."

Rearranging Our Particles

When you play, you *rearrange your particles*. It hurts a little and feels a little good, but it moves you out of where you are. Play takes the snow globe of your life and turns it upside down so that both the environment — and you in it — are changed.

In the past few years, the world has been buzzing with scientific news that the Higgs boson, a.k.a. the "God particle," has finally been found. It is the long-sought-after completion piece to the standard physics model of the entire universe and is considered one of the biggest scientific discoveries in quantum physics, as well as in all of history.

Quantum physicists live in the Skip phase. Like the particles they study, they move in infinite directions, often with no clear destination in sight. Their work reaches the aspects of life that don't make any sense to anyone. I once heard a physicist say that even quantum physicists don't know what quantum physics is! This field holds the numinous mysteries, where rules are broken, common sense is nonexistent, and everything science *thinks* it understands is rearranged. Quantum physics is the ultimate experience of play; Skipping is the ultimate way to rearrange your particles.

TRY THIS: QUANTUM PLAY

1. Look at a typical week. What activities do you spend the most time engaged in? Sort these activities into three to five general categories.

2. Take your list, and write it as an imaginary scientific formula that represents your life. Take the first letter of each item in your list and use it as a variable in the formula. You're writing a formula that doesn't make sense, much like a child who was "playing scientist" would do. See the sidebar for an example of how I did it.

3. Identify some kind of *new* play you'd like to add to your life — something you are not already doing right now. It might be something you've enjoyed in the past but haven't done in a while. Again, using the first letter of the words as variables, add this new element to your equation and play around to see what might happen as a result. As you can see in the sidebar, when I added

the new element, the entire formula shifted. Just playing around with this made-up format made my own inner particles start dancing.

SAMPLE QUANTUM PLAY

My initial list looked like this:

DAY-TO-DAY ACTIVITIES:
Work (teaching, writing, mentoring)
Parenting (games, bedtimes, playtime, homeschool)
Self-care (sleep, green smoothies, exercise)
Fun (quick collages, girls' nights, decorating projects)

Here's my first formula. It looks complicated, but all I did was take the first letter of each word and turn it into an element in the formula. Getting plenty of sleep is really important to me, so that is why I raised it to the tenth power!

$$DtDA = W(t, w, m) + P(g, b, p, h) + SC(s^{10}, gs, e) + F(qc, gn, dp)$$

For my second formula, I decided to add music (piano, singing, composing, simple performance) as the new element, as I haven't been enjoying making music as much as I would like. I followed the rules I vaguely remember from math class and placed the original formula in square brackets, then added the new elements to it. The result? I said that it all equaled joy and an increase in momentum!

$$M(p, s, c, sp) + [W(t, w, m) + P(g, b, p, h) + SC(s^{10}, gs, e) + F(qc, gn, dp)] = Joy \Rightarrow Momentum$$

My particles are now sufficiently shifted, and I feel much smarter than I really am. I can't wait to hang *this* over the piano!

HAIKOODLE

play as quantum cells
baffling the world's brightest minds
who knows how it works?

45 **It's Center Time!**

FUN FACT: Kermit the Frog is left-handed.

*Use your nondominant hand to draw a map of the area
in which you most often work and play.*

When we lived in Hawaii, my sister came to visit us. Tony — ever the good host — filled the drawer next to her bed with chocolates and a few goodies. I remember one evening, we all said good night, and only moments later, she bolted back into the living room and said, "My center has been replenished!" I thought she was just overcome by the beauty of the island, but it actually was because Tony put more chocolates into the little drawer. Since then, "My center has been replenished" has become a favorite playful phrase between us.

Going Back to Kindergarten

When Skipping, you really *do* need to replenish your center, and do it often. One way to do this is to be aware of the places in which you lose energy. In the Skip phase, two of the biggest concerns are time and space. A playful way to approach your various Skipping spaces is to return to your "center" by going back to the centers of kindergarten. Many preschool and kindergarten classrooms are organized by centers — separate areas devoted to different projects. I remember that center time was my favorite part of kindergarten because it was the ultimate in five-year-old freedom: center time meant I could go anywhere I wanted, and even switch from project to project within a given time slot.

As someone naturally inclined to Jump, I admit that I even have a hard time waiting for paint to dry when I'm working on a painting. Setting up separate areas in my studio for different projects — like the kindergarten centers of my wee youth — helped me find the joy of Skipping from one project to another. I found that I could work on multiple projects at once and my paints wouldn't run together from my muddy impatience.

TRY THIS: MAP YOUR CENTERS

Grab your crayons and draw a kindergarten-esque map of the centers of your life. If possible, use a large piece of poster board or butcher paper so you can write and draw using really big shapes and letters. Where do you spend your time and energy? Begin with the projects that are getting the most attention in your life right now, and draw big shapes to represent them in your map. Then think of the new projects that you would like to bring into your life. What would be really fun and feel worthwhile to explore? Draw symbols in your map to represent these projects as well. Use lots of colors and have fun!

Seeing the various projects in your life represented in this way, what do you notice about your map? Is the scale correct, or would you prefer some items to be bigger than others? Are there any centers that need to be moved to be closer together? Is there something you'd like to remove altogether?

HAIKOODLE

play as the bright rug
welcomes kids to story time
listening page by page

46 Either/Oracles

FUN FACT: The Magic 8 Ball offers ten affirmative, five negative, and five neutral responses.

Think of a question on your mind right now.
What are ten affirmative ways you might answer it?

racles are all around us. Even if you've never visited a psychic or fortune-teller, you have certainly been exposed to many oracles. Go to almost any bookstore or stationery shop, and you will see a whole pile of card decks and books that detail ancient oracular traditions, such as the *I Ching*, tarot, runes, and astrology. No matter how skeptical you are about such things, you've probably engaged in a fortune-cookie reading at some point in your life. My client Sheila Masson says, "We live in an oracular universe." Oracles are containers. They hold a different perspective on our dreams, wishes, and ideas.

Playing with Our Choices

People who are very comfortable in the Skipping phase are used to moving from project to project, idea to idea, without a lot of worry. They don't spend time or energy making decisions about what they want to do next; they just follow their instincts. If you are not used to Skipping, but want to activate Skip energy, you can try some experimental ways to approach decision making and see if it takes you to new places.

Allow yourself to play with an oracle. Flip a coin. Draw an angel card. Do a search for "online divination tool," and pick a virtual card. When you play this way, you find new insight. Oracles help you see that you know more than you think. It doesn't matter if you believe you are getting information from a divine source, if you're curiously open to synchronicities, or if you're simply using the oracle as a prompt for expanding your current thinking. It doesn't matter what you believe at all; if you let it, the oracle *will* take you somewhere.

TRY THIS: EASY ORACLES

1. Write down three different projects, activities, or interests that you have right now.
2. For each item on your list, formulate one question — for example:

   What am I not seeing about the fund-raising event?
   How can I get a better idea of how to approach writing my novel?
   What would be the best way to tackle mowing the lawn to make it more fun?

3. Access a free online oracle, with a Google search. Follow the directions for the oracle, keeping one of your questions in mind.
4. What has playing with this oracle shown you? How have you been brought to new information? How has your imagination been awakened in this type of play?

HAIKOODLE

play as oracle
ask and you'll get an answer
a child understands

{ Don't forget to doodle }

47 Grounding in Play

FUN FACT: In the mid-nineteenth century, sand gardens became the first organized and supervised playgrounds in America.

What was your favorite part of the playground when you were a child? How might it be relevant to your dream?

The word *playground* is one of my favorite playful words because it includes a delightful message: you *ground* in play. This is important because sometimes play can feel frivolous or fru-fru, jivrulous or ju-ju, quivrulous or qu-qu. Granted, someone who just used the made-up word "jivrulous" in a sentence may not seem like the most grounded gal in the world, but she's not qu-qu either. Play lets us fly high, but it also can keep us close to the ground.

Energetic Grounding

The chakra system is a body-energy science that dates back to the eighth century. Chakras are energy points that connect to different parts of the body; through each chakra, you access a particular channel of personal core energy. When energetic channels are blocked, internal beliefs become stuck, and external actions become stagnant. As medical intuitive and author Caroline Myss explains, "Every thought and experience you've ever had in your life gets filtered through these chakra databases. Each event is recorded into your cells." The base chakra — also called the root chakra — is the area related to basic survival. It is the energy channel that roots the body and soul to the earth. It is the source of *grounding*.

Feeling a lack of grounding is very common during the Skip phase. When your energies are pulling you in a lot of different directions, it is easy to lose the tether to your purpose and overall direction. When you lose your grounding, you lose the feeling of your feet in the soil.

The great outdoors is wonderful for getting back to a sense of connection and oneness. Spending time outdoors helps you connect to the fullness of life and the little details you miss if you don't look closely enough.

TRY THIS: BUILD AN IMPROMPTU PLAYGROUND

1. Go on a nature walk with child's eyes. Challenge yourself to make *all* of your senses more open and aware and allow yourself to be drawn into the magical experience of playing in nature.
2. Gather interesting leaves, rocks, little flowers, and other pieces of nature.
3. Take the elements you've gathered and make a playground for little fairies, dragonflies, or other small creatures. What do you design? Does the leaf turn into a slide? Is the twig a climbing poll? Are all the little acorn tops set up in a circle like a merry-go-round?
4. After your playground is done, take a step back and look at it. What does it tell you about the projects you are working on right now? Are there any similarities between this mini-environment and your own life right now? Do you get any new insights about your various projects, ideas, and interests? Most important, how do you *feel* now that you've spent some time outdoors touching

Mother Nature with your hands? You might want to take a photo of the playground to continue to inspire you.

5. Leave the playground where it is so the fairies and dragonflies can find it.

HAIKOODLE

play as a playground
swing, slide, sandbox, jungle gym
small city of bliss

TOP TEN SIGNS YOU NEED TO TAKE A BREAK AND GROUND YOUR ENERGY

10. You're trying to send a text message using the TV remote control.
9. Adding an appointment to your calendar reminds you of playing Tetris.
8. You find yourself ordering a sandwich from the bank teller.
7. You notice your shoes don't match — but not until the very end of the day.
6. You've forgotten what you're reading right now.
5. The last time you took a really deep breath was in the doctor's office during your annual physical.
4. Your last annual physical was three years ago.
3. You brushed your teeth with hand cream last night.
2. You find your car by wandering through the streets, pressing the "unlock" button.
1. You greet close friends by saying, "I don't think we've met."

48 Completion and Candy Hearts

FUN FACT: Johnny Gruelle's original Raggedy Ann had a real candy heart sewn inside her, and the creator's son, Worth Gruelle, says he remembers his family sewing candy hearts into the original dolls.

If you were to give a candy heart to your dream,
what message would be written on it?

When I was pregnant, I started making a Christmas stocking for the baby. I bought a pattern and thought it would be a lovely craft that I could complete for the baby's first Christmas the next year. You have probably already guessed that the stocking was never finished. I don't think I even touched it again after that Great-with-Child year; in fact, I actually have no idea where it is now. I'm hoping it is at least providing a nice home to a cute little mouse somewhere. As I recall from watching the animated classic *The Night before Christmas*, mice need happy Christmases, too!

Trusting Your Skip

In the Skip phase, you *won't* complete everything you start. In fact, that is what the Skip phase is all about; accepting Skipping as an independent phase of manifestation allows us to trust that our unfinished projects have gotten us somewhere important and that we can choose when we want to Jump.

When you *don't* fully appreciate the Skip phase, it can do a real number on your self-esteem. I have worked with clients who define themselves negatively by their unfinished projects. "I just look around and see that I've *started* so many things, but I never finish *anything*," Jen says. "I just do everything in this halfhearted, incomplete way. I feel like all these projects are just looking at me, sticking out their tongues, and telling me that I'm a loser."

If you can relate to Jen's words, now is the time to play with the *fullness* of each of these half-ish projects. There is nothing halfhearted about Skipping; after all, the physical act of skipping is the time when your heart is engaged more fully than when you are hopping or jumping. With a new perspective, you may see that many of these projects actually already *are* complete, in that you have gotten what you needed from them. You can trust the process and the gifts that Skipping gives you. You can trust yourself and your own manifesting skills. So if you are sitting with a lot of unfinished projects, that means you are doing the Skipping phase *right*.

TRY THIS: TRANSFORMING HALFHEARTEDNESS

1. Cut out a bunch of paper hearts by folding pieces of paper in half and cutting a half-heart shape. Do not unfold them yet.
2. Pick up one of the folded hearts, and write one of your unfinished projects on one side of it.
3. Turn the half heart over, and on the opposite side, write, doodle, and draw the ways in which this project has helped you. Did you learn something new? Did you have fun? Did you get to make a new connection as a result?
4. Open the heart to see the fullness of it. There is nothing "half" about this project. It has given you exactly what you needed.
5. Repeat for the other hearts. After you have a set of hearts,

lay them out in front of you. Try to discern which projects really *are* complete because you've gotten everything you need from them. On the other hand, see which hearts are rapidly beating for your attention. Where does your energy want to go? Which hearts are ready to make the leap?

ACROWHIM
HEARTS = Here, Eternal Affection Runs The Show

HAIKOODLE

play as cutout heart
unfolds a mirror image
reflects who I am

49 Merry-Go-Round Manifestation

FUN FACT: Fewer than twenty pre-1960 vintage carousels in North America still have operating brass-ring dispensers or targets.

The phrase "grabbing the brass ring" refers to striving for life's highest prize. What is your definition of fully enjoying life?

T*he Wizard of Oz* helps grown-ups feel like kids again. I recently watched the whole film from start to finish and found myself not only being touched by my own nostalgic memories, but genuinely enjoying the movie. Inspired to do some research about the making of the movie, I became even more impressed, learning about the pioneering ways that the film's special effects were created. Did you know that when the Wicked Witch tries to touch Dorothy's slippers, the electric-bolt effect that appears to be coming out of her hands was created by shooting apple juice out of the shoes and speeding up the film? Spewing apple juice is something Kai used to do at the kitchen table every day, and I never knew it could be considered a special effect.

Catching the Brass Ring

This year, I cotaught a fourteen-week online seminar for aspiring authors with Marc Allen, cofounder and publisher of New

World Library and one of my favorite manifesting visionaries. He introduced me to these words of comedian Bert Lahr (who played the Lion in *The Wizard of Oz*), which summarize the role of perseverance in the Skip phase: "Stay on the merry-go-round long enough, and you're bound to catch the brass ring sooner or later."

It used to be a tradition for carousel operators to toss out rings for riders to catch during the ride. Typically, there was a large number of iron rings and one brass one, and catching the brass ring usually meant getting a prize or another ride free. *The moment when you move from the Skip to the Jump stage is the moment right before you catch the brass ring.*

When you are enjoying the carousel ride, you aren't worried about a goal. But when you can feel yourself leaning forward to try to catch that brass ring, you know you are getting ready to Jump. This is a sensation you can feel in your body. It might show up as a kind of tension; you're no longer just sitting back and enjoying. But it's an *excited* kind of tension. You sit a little taller, poised and ready. You reach out your hands. When you miss it; it's no problem. You get another chance. As Lahr said, if you stay on long enough, you'll catch it eventually, as long as you keep your hands out.

When Kai makes a poor behavior choice — say, flinging apple juice from his hands — he will beg dramatically, "Please, one last chance!" In the Skipping phase, you continually get new chances without even asking for them. Every moment is a new moment as you go round and round. Keep riding; keep reaching for the brass ring. You have been given the birthright to reach out and try again. And again.

TRY THIS: RIDING AND WRITING THE CAROUSEL

1. Draw a carousel, or something that might represent a carousel. Don't worry if your carousel looks like an amoeba or a pizza; remember, this is not about drawing skill.

2. Draw a bunch of rings that are being tossed around. Label each ring with an idea, project, or activity that you've been enjoying lately.

3. Take a look at all the rings, and see if you can get a sense of which one might be brass — the one that is shiny and truly drawing your attention. If you had to pick just one, which one would you pick?

4. Add *yourself* to that picture, grabbing the ring. What do your body and your facial expression look like in your picture? More important, how do you feel when you are drawing? Does it feel right? Are you ready, or would you rather keep riding for a bit? There is no right or wrong answer to this question. But if you think you might be ready, then it might be time to Jump!

MANIFESTAGRAM
Riding the carousel = Oracle: I end us right.

HAIKOODLE

play as carousel
riding while you stay in place
you travel for miles

50   Play and Pinwheels

FUN FACT: Toy pinwheels are also referred to as "whirligigs."

Invent a new dance called "the whirligig." What does the dance look like, and on what occasion is it introduced?

As the friendly narrator of this little play, I'm starting to get a bit nervous. Here we are, at the end of the Skip phase, and I fear you may be wanting me to tell you, "This will be *so* easy, dear reader! You'll *never* struggle! If you've prepared yourself with ample Hopping and Skipping, the Jumping will be a breeze! Here's how…"

And then, of course, I'd give you a series of easy steps to make it so.

Sadly, I can't give you the secret for making it a breeze. However, I *can* share that a *breeze* is, in many ways, the secret for moving from Skipping to Jumping.

The Importance of Inspiration

Your manifestation process is a lot like a child playing with a pinwheel. The child has to keep blowing to keep the pinwheel going, so she blows and blows. When she stops, the pinwheel stops. This continues until eventually a wind comes through, and suddenly the colors spin without effort.

Of course, it takes patience to provide that stream of air to keep the pinwheel in motion until something bigger than your own effort keeps it moving. You have two choices: you can sit around and wait for the wind, becoming increasingly exhausted and depleted, or you can *enjoy* the spinning, dancing colors, the playful moment. In other words, when you're blowing the pinwheel, you need to make sure that your breath is not just flowing out, but coming *in* as well.

The literal meaning of the word *inspire* is "to breathe in." As you transition from the Skip to the Jump phase, you get to remember to *keep yourself inspired*. Your ability to sustain the exhalation to move the pinwheel comes from momentum and belief — the belief that you *can* do this, and that the wind *will* come in so you won't have to do it alone.

To stay inspired, you must believe that the world needs your pinwheel to spin. Remember, in times of global change and uncertainty, it isn't the stuffy corporate executives packing their pockets with their exorbitant salaries and self-serving back deals who will help our economy rise back up on its feet again or who will fill our hearts with hope. The people who are going to be the catalysts of change will be the steadfast, nurturing weavers of wisdom; the illuminating, passionate painters of purpose; and the encouraging, persistent handcrafters of hope. The world *needs* you to play.

It doesn't matter *what* you are manifesting. Even if you are manifesting something very simple, you can use your playful power to elevate the importance of it to something broader and wider. One person playfully manifesting a meaningful life makes a difference. As Howard Thurman said, "Don't ask what the world needs. Ask what makes you come alive, and go do it. Because what the world needs is people who have come alive." You are making a difference. The world *needs* you to keep your pinwheel moving as the winds of change blow through us all.

1. Buy a pinwheel at a dollar store, or use your crayons to draw a pinwheel.

2. On the pieces of the pinwheel, write reasons why what you are manifesting is important for the world. If you are using an actual pinwheel, a permanent marker ought to work nicely.

3. Use this image to elevate the importance of your project or goal. When you keep your pinwheel spinning, you help the world spin; you are part of the web of life, doing your part. Whenever you need inspiration, look at your pinwheel and take in a deep breath. And then use the inspiration from within to exhale, and watch the pinwheel move.

ACROWHIM

PINWHEEL = Perpetual Inspiration Needs Whimsy to Hold Energetic Emotion Lovingly

HAIKOODLE

play as a pinwheel
trying to mix up the air
the wind's masterpiece

SECTION THREE

JUMP

51
Transitioning on the Tightrope

FUN FACT: Pixar movies contain many references to one another. For example, in *Toy Story 3*, we see a postcard from the couple from the movie *Up*, and Buzz Lightyear uses B&L batteries, which is the corporation from *WALL-E*.

What is the name of the batteries that you use to propel yourself into action?

Now we move into the Jump phase, in which we consciously move our dream into action and focus on bringing it to completion. This is where some people think, "Oh, now the fun is over, and the work starts. There's no way that *this* part can be fun." If you're feeling some hesitation moving into action, then you might want to revisit the Play-To Philosophy from chapter 1 to remember that *you* have a choice as to whether something feels serious or fun, laborious or easy, work or play. All the exercises you've been doing up to this point have been great practice, because now you know exactly what play feels like, and how easy it really can be to enter into a playful space. As mentioned previously, one of the key aspects of play for children is the way that play helps them practice for the future. Although I must agree with my client, Jane, who pointed out that it seems utterly ridiculous to give children pretend cleaning tools: plastic vacuum cleaners, brooms, and dustpans. We could just give them the real thing and enjoy the few years of free labor!

The Real Thing

The problem is that we, as grown-ups, are often so comfortable rehearsing something in our minds that we hold ourselves back from actually *doing* it. We plan, imagine, and mentally rehearse our vision. This definitely gets our dreams activated, but it doesn't get our dreams *actualized*. Eventually, something moves us from "toying" around with things to actually taking action. Something inside us becomes bigger than the safety of the status quo.

When we are grounded in play, this transition needn't be jarring. Richard Bach said, "The more I want to get something done, the less I call it work." Of course, when you approach the Jump phase with a playful attitude, it doesn't mean that suddenly everything you do will be sunshine and roses, but it *does* mean that you will be primed to look for the places where you find ease and joy. As long as you understand this, you can enter into the "real thing" with consciousness, enthusiasm, and, especially, a sense of *balance*.

The concept of balance is often misunderstood. Many folks feel that if they are focused and disciplined, upbeat and positive, loving and generous, healthy and energetic...then they will be balanced. But balance is *not* about walking around with a bunch of "positive," happy qualities; balance is about walking the tightrope between the polarities within us as well as the tightropes among the circumstances outside us.

In photography, we can't even see an image unless its negative — its opposite — is included. In life, balance means that you not only accept the "negatives," but actually *use* them to create the whole picture.

> ### TRY THIS: ROMP TO THE REAL THING

This is kind of like a "mad lib," where you fill in the blanks of a story. Think of something you associate with the "pretend version" and the "real thing" — two items you can compare with one another in terms of their authenticity. For example, you might compare a low-carb, low-fat chai latte versus an authentic, creamy chai latte; a knockoff purse versus a designer handbag; artificial flowers versus a real bouquet; or a Yule log video versus an actual roaring fire. The items you pick needn't have anything to do with your dream or what you want to manifest. You can use one of the examples given above or come up with your own.

1. Write about your experience with these two things by filling in the blanks in the following paragraph:

   [Pretend version] and [real thing] are different. I notice that [pretend version] is _____, while [real thing] is _____. [Pretend version] just isn't the same as [real thing] because _____. [Real thing] makes me feel _____, and when I'm experiencing it, I know it's real because _____.

   When writing this paragraph, feel free to add anything that describes the way you distinguish the pretend version from the real thing.

2. Put your paragraph aside, and then bring your attention to your dream. Complete the following two sentences about your dream or whatever you want to manifest, by replacing the *a* and *b*:

   I have been toying with *a*.
   But now I am committing to *b*.

3. Now take the paragraph you wrote in step 1, and rewrite it by replacing the pretend version and real thing with "toying with *a*" and "committing to *b*" (using the words you used in step 2 for *a* and *b*). The topics of the two paragraphs will be completely different, and you may have to make some small tweaks so that the new paragraph makes sense. Your new paragraph will read something like this:

Toying with *a* and committing to *b* are different. I notice that toying with *a* is [words you used in step 1], while committing to *b* is [words you used in step 1]. Toying with *a* just isn't the same as committing to *b* because [words you used in step 1]. Committing to *b* makes me feel [words you used in step 1], and when I'm experiencing it, I know it's real because [words you used in step 1].

What do you notice in your rewrite of the paragraph? Do you see anything new that makes your dream feel more real in your life? Is there a new perspective that offers a shift in thinking or a new motivation for taking action?

See the sidebar for an example of my two paragraphs and the resulting insights.

MANIFESTAGRAM
The real thing = Higher talent

HAIKOODLE

play as chai latte
in an oversize teacup
peace within the steam

EXAMPLE OF MY "ROMP TO THE REAL THING"

Here is my first paragraph, where I compare a low-carb, low-fat chai latte with an authentic chai latte:

> A low-carb, low-fat chai latte and an authentic chai latte are different. I notice that the low-carb version is sweet and tasty but a bit watery, while the authentic chai latte is more complete. The low-carb version just isn't the same as the full version because I don't get that same sense of deep comfort and luxuriousness. The authentic chai latte makes me feel alive and awake and I want to take my time with it, and when I'm experiencing it, I know it's real because I really feel like I am giving myself a treat.

In rewriting the paragraph, I made my replacements using "toying with the idea of getting in shape" and "committing to hire a personal trainer." Here is my second story:

> Toying with the idea of getting in shape and committing to hire a personal trainer are different. I notice that toying with the idea of getting in shape is sweet and tasty but a bit watery, while committing to hire a personal trainer is more complete. Toying with the idea of getting in shape just isn't the same as committing to hire a personal trainer because I don't get that same sense of deep comfort and luxuriousness. Committing to hire a personal trainer makes me feel alive and awake and I want to take my time with it, and when I'm experiencing it, I know it's real because I really feel like I am giving myself a treat.

When I read back the second paragraph, the new perspective I get is that committing to hire a personal trainer can feel deeply comfortable and luxurious, like a special treat. Prior to doing this exercise, toying with the idea felt like the safe choice, while committing to getting a trainer felt scary and perhaps a bit too bold. Romping through this exercise helped me see that the commitment to hiring a trainer could actually be the safer, more comforting choice. Who knew? It's a whole new perspective that can help me take the leap from *toying* to *trying*, from an idea to action . . . from Skipping to Jumping!

52   The Zoomie Car Game

FUN FACT: One of the predecessors of reality TV was the *Up* series, a series of documentary films that follows the lives of fourteen British children, beginning when they were seven years old in 1964. Every seven years, they have released a new film featuring the individuals, the latest showing them at age fifty-four. The premise of the original film was taken from a quote by Francis Xavier: "Give me a child until he is seven and I will give you the man."

Think back to yourself at seven years old.
What would you say were your predominant qualities?
How do those qualities compare to who you are today?

Perhaps I'm wrong, but I think reality TV began in my childhood bedroom. Whenever I needed to clean my room — which was often — my sister, Launa, would "host" a make-believe game show called *The Zoomie Car Show*. Here's the premise of the game: Two identical bedrooms were set up to be equally messy. I was a contestant going up against another contestant (usually someone from Romania or Russia, inspired by the Nadia-versus-Olga gymnastics rivalry in the 1970s), and we were in a race to see who could finish cleaning the room more quickly. My sister was the announcer who gave a captivating description of all the action. Within her play-by-play, we tapped the *play* I needed to complete the task.

Great Oaks from Little Acorns

The Jump phase is about embracing *completion energy*, which refers to the embodiment and the full experience of completion. Everything you do in the Hop and Skip phases prepares you for completion. But even so…when you do finally get to the Jump phase, it can still feel a little overwhelming as you see the *bigness* of what you set out to do. That's a big grant application to write. That's a huge degree to earn. That's a lot of weight to lose. That's a *really* messy room to clean.

The old proverb "Great oaks from little acorns grow" reminds us of the potential destiny of small starts. It is easier to make a small movement than a large one. Deepak Chopra calls this the "Law of Least Effort." This is important when we look at the energetics of action.

What if you were on a reality-TV show and were told you would win a million dollars if you could open an independent bookstore in your town and make a profit within three months. With stakes *that* high, I imagine you probably would feel a bit overwhelmed. But what if, instead, you were told you'd win only one thousand dollars if you simply did three things:

1. Look up independent bookstores in your area to see what already exists.
2. Invite one owner of an existing store to lunch, to hear a bit about his experience.
3. Make a list of questions you'd like to ask him.

No problem, right?

What if you were then told you'd get *another* thousand dollars if you did another three steps. And then another thousand for another set of three after that?

When you break things down into units that do *not* feel

overwhelming, the units can build on each other. This lesson is repeated in nature, science, and psychology: it is by breaking things down that we are able to build them up.

And, lastly, if anyone out there wants to produce *The Zoomie Car Show*, Launa and I are ready to serve as consultants.

TRY THIS: PRODUCE YOUR REALITY SHOW

1. What is your big goal? Pretend that you are producing a reality-TV show in which the person who *completes* this goal wins $1,000,000. What is the name of the show, and how does it work?

2. Now produce a second show, in which $1,000 prizes are given for doing three steps at a time. What do the steps consist of? What is the name of this show? Plan the first three episodes.

3. Produce a third show, this time awarding $333.33 for doing just *one* step. What is the name of *this* show? Plan the first three episodes.

4. What do you notice from your stint as a reality-show producer? Which show was easiest to produce? What can you take away from this experience to inspire your own action steps in real life?

ACROWHIM
ACTION = Answering Calls To Initiate
Opportunities Now

HAIKOODLE

play as baby steps
a wobbly experiment
toddlers don't give up

53 Your Easy-Bake Oven

FUN FACT: The original Kenner Easy-Bake Oven was heated by two one-hundred-watt lightbulbs, a design inspired by the roasted chestnuts sold by street vendors in New York City.

How will you know when your idea
or project is fully baked?
Can you test it for doneness,
like sticking a toothpick in a cake?

I never had an Easy-Bake Oven; but I had friends who did, and it was so fun to see what happened when we would bake our little concoctions. As I recall, they tasted like cardboard, but as kids, we didn't care. It was so gratifying to look at something and say, "I did this!"

The Easy-Bake Oven makes me think of those times when you're moving along and suddenly find yourself stuck with nowhere to turn but to the Dreaded Task in Front of You. Frustrated and craving non-cardboard-ish chocolate cake, you realize that you have no choice but to start from scratch, roll up your sleeves, and do what you have to do. Believe it or not, this is a great time to play!

Playing with New Recipes

A big difference between the Skip and the Jump phase is that in Jumping, you *will* be doing some things that aren't naturally fun. There will be action steps that are *foundational* (that is, other actions depend on them) and *immediate* (that is, a timeline is dependent on their completion). In the Skip phase, you don't have to worry about foundational or immediate actions; if you encounter resistance, you get to just follow your energy somewhere else. That is how you keep your momentum going while Skipping. However, when you are truly committed to Jumping, then you'll need another strategy to find some play in the sticky, not-so-cooked parts.

Karen was very excited about self-publishing a set of cards from her art. However, there was a foundational action she needed to face: going through tutorials for a new digital art program. It was something she had been content to put off while Skipping, but once she had fully claimed herself in the Jump phase, Karen knew it was time to face it. So we looked for her *portal to play* to make this dreaded task more appealing. In order for this to work, she had to throw out her old associations with the task and be willing to *start from scratch*.

One helpful way to start from scratch is to play with a new *name* for your task. In Karen's case, I suggested renaming "tutorials" to become "tuliporials." Having landed on this new name, she suddenly saw many possibilities: buying tulips to put by her computer; letting herself "tiptoe" through the material, going easy on herself, rather than stomping through it; taking time to stop and smell each tulip as she went through the modules. With this new word, she could start from scratch, with new ingredients.

TRY THIS: START FROM SCRATCH WITH A DREADED TASK

1. Pick a dreaded task that is either foundational or immediate. Use the appropriate one of these phrases, and fill

in the blank with a short description of the task (for example, "finish the tutorials"):

> For a foundational task: "I know that sooner or later, I'll need to _____ even though I'm dreading it."
>
> For an immediate task: "I am on a firm deadline to _____, and I really wish I didn't have to."

2. Look at the description you wrote in the blank in step 1, and pick out the main word in the description (for example, *tutorials* in "finish the tutorials"). Separate yourself from what this word means or what it represents, and just *look at the word itself*. What does this word remind you of? What other word might you see in it, such as *tulips* in the word *tutorials*? Is there a rhyme or a shift in the letters that reveals another word? Try to create two or three new words.

3. Look at the new words you've created, and then explore what each of them might mean. Fill in the blanks in the following template to help yourself discover how each *new* word and its meaning might affect your approach:

> I get to [new word], and that sounds kind of fun!
> [New word] might mean _____.
> It might mean _____.
> It might mean _____.
> (You can continue and list as many meanings as you like.)
> My first step is _____.

See the sidebar for an example of this technique.

MANIFESTAGRAM
Easy-bake treats = Eat baker's yeast.

EXAMPLE OF STARTING FROM SCRATCH
WITH A DREADED TASK

My dreaded task was filing paperwork with a health insurance company. This task felt tedious and overwhelming, but I knew that, sooner or later, I had to do it.

When I looked at the word *file*, I saw the word *filly*. The image of a young female horse was intriguing, though I hadn't a clue what it meant. Here is what I got when I completed the Start from Scratch with a Dreaded Task process:

I get to *filly*, and that sounds kind of fun!

Filly might mean to call on my feminine side while I'm going through the paperwork.

It might mean I take small trots instead of big gallops during this task.

It might mean to focus on the "mane" task and not get distracted.

It might mean that combing through papers could be an act of love — I could tenderly groom the paperwork and attend to it with care and fondness.

It might mean tapping into the abundant feeling of being in the caretaker role for this task and feeling grateful for the opportunity.

It might mean doing something feminine and "frilly" as part of the task, like decorating the submission envelope with whimsical, hand-drawn ribbons and bows.

My first step is to take the disorganized stack of papers and very gingerly sort them into appropriate piles, gently smoothing each paper with appreciation and wonderment as I do so.

Going from being overwhelmed to a feeling of true gratitude and care — plus ribbons and bows — is a really significant shift for me, especially when it comes to an unpleasant task like filing paperwork! I'm off to groom my stack of papers. Would you like to join me?

HAIKOODLE

play as recipes
instructions, ingredients
typed on a dance card

TOP TEN SIGNS
YOU MIGHT NOT BE A KITCHEN WIZARD

10. You always burn the Jell-O.
9. You watch cooking shows at night to put you to sleep.
8. You confuse a sauté with that thing in European bathrooms.
7. Your pot holders are currently being used as wall art.
6. You've wrapped store-bought cookies in cute little bags for more than one homemade-cookie swap.
5. You've never made anything from scratch except boiled water.
4. Your first thought when you hear "extra-virgin olive oil" is "Popeye, the adult-film version."
3. Let's not be modest — you make a mean microwave pop-corn.
2. The Play-Doh meals prepared by your child look tastier than your actual meals.
1. Your friends always ask you to bring the ice.

54   Just Haiku It

FUN FACT: In 1907, in Japan, education scholar Minoru Wada published a groundbreaking article about *yudo-hoiku* that introduced the concept of a child-centered education for preschoolers based on free play. Today, it is still regarded as one of the most important preschool education studies.

The word hoiku *means "playful education" or "the education of a young child." What are you currently learning or studying, and how could this education be more playful?*

Throughout this book you've been haikoodling and doodling. I love haiku because it is fun and easy, and offers such a simple, doable structure for poetry. In *Creating Time*, I begin each chapter with a "poetic pause" — a haiku that invites the reader to change the tempo of reading rather than rushing through the book, which serves an important function in a book about reinventing our relationship with time. We metabolize poetry differently than prose, and it changes the way we read words.

I have to be honest, though, and confess that there is absolutely nothing altruistic about the Haikoodles in this book; they are here for *my own* sense of play. Whenever the writing felt like work, I'd write a Haikoodle for a chapter or two, and that would give me the little zip of energy I needed to get back in the flow. The Haikoodles helped me Jump through this book, and that is why you have it in your hands right now.

The Element of Fun

Let's keep things real: during the Jump phase, you *will* come across actions that don't feel fun. You might remember the old *Mary Poppins* song about a spoonful of sugar; well, haiku is one of my favorite ways to find that element of fun — in seventeen sweet syllables of sugar.

TRY THIS: CREATING A HAIKU SOLUTION

The traditional structure of haiku is three lines: the first line has five syllables; the second line has seven syllables; the third line has five syllables.

Here's a format you can play with, using haiku as a playful way to help you find a new solution:

- Five syllables to represent the dreaded task
- Seven syllables to represent how you are feeling
- Five syllables to represent your next step

See the sidebar for an example of this format.

At the very least, even if no earth-shattering solutions arise, you *will* shift your energy by taking two minutes to write a poem. It's easier to go back to the task at hand when you've mixed things up a bit. Now excuse me while I go write a haiku...

ACROWHIM
HAIKU = Hold An Insight; Keep Unveiling

HAIKOODLE

play as a poem
wondering, "Does this make sense?"
the metaphor nods

55 Priorities and Glorities

FUN FACT: Tinkertoys were invented by Charles Pajeau, who got the idea while watching kids play with pencils, sticks, and empty spools of thread.

What might it look like to "tinker" with your goals and priorities? In what ways might that be different from your normal approach?

The very word *priorities* often makes people shrivel into a litany of old beliefs like:

- I don't know how to prioritize.
- Everything is equally important.
- I procrastinate too much.
- I don't have it in me to succeed.

Which old beliefs come up for you?

Shifting Your Story about Priorities

Because we don't like the word *priorities*, my husband, Tony, and I made up a different word: *glorities*. Once again, simply playfully shifting a word makes a huge difference.

We now use this word exclusively and have even taken to using it with members of the Artella team. Sometimes "glorities" make everyone breathe a little easier. It's so much nicer to see the word "Glority" in the subject line of an email than a red exclamation mark that's screaming self-importance.

Here is the difference:

- *Priorities* means choosing what is important.
- *Glorities* means choosing what is glorious and alive.

When you call your most important things "glorities," you align with a new set of beliefs: My work is glorious. My forward movement is glorious. I am glorious.

TRY THIS: WRITE YOUR GLORY STORY

Here is a playful way to see your current priorities in a different light. It's called a "glory story." Put your name in the first blank, and then continue by filling in the blanks with the first words that come to mind. Don't think too much about your answers; just write the words that pop into your mind first, even if they don't seem to make a lot of sense. If appropriate, replace "girl" with "boy," "she" with "he," and so on.

Once upon a time, there was a little girl named
_____. She tried so hard to reach her
goal of _____, but no matter how hard she
tried, she _____. When pushed onto the
Pathway of Priorities, she felt _____,
and she found herself _____. This
made her feel _____.

One day, she decided to leave the Pathway of Priorities because she finally realized _____. She looked around and saw _____. She then noticed the Garden of Glorities. It looked like _____. It was there she found _____.

She found the glory of _____.
She found the glory of _____.
She found the glory of _____.

Once she found the magic Garden of Glorities, she finally understood _____ _____.

And she knew that her next step was to _____.

The End

What does your story tell you? What new insights, energies, or ideas are revealed?

MANIFESTAGRAM
New priorities = "Inspire," I wrote.

HAIKOODLE

play as flower beds
perennial wake-up calls
from morning glories

56

Hula Hoops
and
Loop-de-Loops

If you could make a hula hoop to help your ideas stay in motion, what materials would you use?

When I was living on the Big Island of Hawaii, I enjoyed watching hula dance performances regularly. Hula is a profoundly beautiful art in which the body is used to tell a story, and because I've seen it executed with such perfection and reverence, I've been too intimidated to try it myself. However, I recently heard there is something called the "hula hoop workout," which is an exercise class that uses hula hoops. While hula dancing still feels intimidating to me, a hula hoop just feels like fun, so I'm definitely willing to try that — *that's* work as play!

Open Hoops and Loops

While the Skip phase encouraged you to keep your possibilities open, the Jump phase is all about *identifying and closing openings where energy is leaking out.* Imagine a paper chain of links, with some open and some closed. Now imagine trying to spin that chain around you like a playful hula hoop. It wouldn't work! The open links would slip out, and the chain would fall apart.

Here in the Jump phase, you get to identify any open loops that may be leaking energy. Time-management expert David Allen says each thing undone on our list is a *broken contract to ourselves* and inhibits our psychic "RAM" (random-access memory). That sounds awfully serious, but there is much truth to it. In the Skip stage, things undone don't matter; in the Jump stage, they *do* matter. However, this doesn't have to feel dismal and foreboding. Let's have some fun closing those loops!

TRY THIS· THE CHAIN GAME

Like the hope rope in chapter 5, this activity uses a paper chain as a playful tool to help track your awareness and progress.

1. Cut strips of paper, and on each strip, use your crayons to write something in your life that is using energy that would be better used somewhere else. This could include outdated projects, cluttered environments, unsupportive relationships, or anything in your life that isn't in full alignment with who you are and what you are manifesting. It could also include actions you need to take or tasks you need to complete.

2. Keep these open slips accessible, to remind you of the open loops in your life. Whenever you "close" a loop, add it to your paper chain, close the loop, and tape the slip together so it becomes a chain link. For example, you might tape a slip together when you complete an unfinished task, release an outdated project, let yourself off the hook for an unhelpful goal, or establish a boundary in an unsupportive relationship. Taping the slip together to become a link symbolizes that energy is contained and completed. The resulting chain will consist not only of things you've done, but of things you have *not* done. It might include things you have *processed* rather than just things you have *produced*.

3. Optional: Try using the fully closed chain as a hula hoop. If that doesn't work, see if your local gym offers a hula hoop workout. Maybe I'll see you there.

ACROWHIM	
LOOPS = Look Out — Open Portals Shrivel	

HAIKOODLE

play as a long chain
link by link creating peace
children holding hands

FUN FACT: The Cloud Appreciation Society's website (www.cloud appreciationsociety.org) includes a gallery of photos, a quiz for advanced cloud watchers, and a cloud selector tool to help identify the clouds.

*Find the nearest sky right now and look for a shape
in the clouds. If no cloud is available, go to the gallery at
www.cloudappreciationsociety.org and pick an image.
What does this image want to tell you about action?*

For years, my husband and I slept on lovely flannel sheets with a bright blue sky and white clouds on them. Like my hero, Mary Poppins, I had always wanted to sit on clouds, the way she does in the opening of the movie. I found it quite relaxing and inspiring to actually get to *sleep* on clouds, until my husband, not the most experienced home arts practitioner, had a snafu with the laundry. Our sheets came out what can only be described as gray sky with gray clouds. He shrugged his shoulders and suggested that now we could sleep on clouds with silver linings. At least he gets an A for effort.

Jumping in the Clouds

"Get your head out of the clouds!" Many heard this message as children and associate it with too much dreaming. Yet, in the Jump phase, the clouds are exactly where your head needs to be. In fact, if you are Jumping and your head is *not* in the clouds, you have not jumped high enough. The act of dreaming — which begins in the Hop phase — continues all the way through to the final Jump.

Imagine, though, that the substance of your blue-sky dreamscapes gets to change a bit when you are in the Jump phase. Here your clouds become *something you can touch* — like whipped cream, white-chocolate mousse, or those fancy-shmancy goosedown pillows that puff up like popovers when you shake them. Here in the Jump phase, your clouds retain their graceful white airiness, but now they have a *moldable* substance. This becomes the special magic property of clouds when you are Jumping through them.

These wonderful words from *Walden* by Henry David Thoreau say so much about the way in which things begin to coalesce in the Jump phase:

> If one advances confidently in the direction of his dreams, and endeavors to live the life which he has imagined, he will meet with a success unexpected in common hours. He will put some things behind, will pass an invisible boundary; new, universal, and more liberal laws will begin to establish themselves around and within him; or the old laws will be expanded, and interpreted in his favor in a more liberal sense, and he will live with the license of a higher order of beings.... If you have built castles in the air, your work need not be lost; that is where they should be. Now put the foundations under them.

These words are the most useful thing I have *ever* read, heard, or practiced that is related to Jumping. No matter how much you have planned or prepared, you *will* hit a time when it feels like you are suspended in the air with nothing underneath you. Suddenly, you will see that your well-thought-out plan didn't work, or realize you skipped a step or forgot something crucial; or perhaps the wind simply changed, and the sky has carried you away from your original, carefully built structures.

When you find yourself in this state, follow Thoreau's advice, which puts it so simply: *now put the foundations under them.* No need to dwell on what went wrong or what didn't happen, on whether it was the wind's fault or yours; stop analyzing and just start building. Nothing up to this point has been wasted. Do what you need to do to get the necessary foundations, all the while being grateful for the solid, sturdy clouds that hold you up in the meantime.

TRY THIS: PAINTING WITH THE CLOUDS

1. Get a can of shaving cream,* whipped cream, or hair mousse. You're going to have some fun! You also need a piece of sturdy paper, a fork, and a place to play where you can get a bit messy.

2. On your sturdy paper, draw a picture of a castle, suspended in the air. Use a marker or crayon to write what you are manifesting on the castle.

3. Next, spray the cream or mousse on your paper, all around your castle, as if you were decorating the scene with magical clouds. Let your inner child have a blast with this. Use the whole can, and really go to town. (Just please do not spray it in your mouth if you're using shaving cream or hair mousse!)

4. Use the fork to make some designs in the clouds around your castle. You can try other design makers as well: toothpicks, coffee stirrers, a plastic comb, a twig. Pretend you are a cloud watcher who can actually *control* the

---

* Advanced version: Add white glue to shaving cream to make a mixture that is "cloud paint," which dries dimensional and puffy.

cloud formations. What do you paint with the clouds, those lovely whipped dreams? In what ways might these clouds become *foundations* under your castle?

5. What insights or ideas came to you while you were playing with the clouds? What did you notice about the foundations under your castle?

MANIFESTAGRAM
A head in the clouds = Delicate nod: a hush

HAIKOODLE

play as fluffy clouds
thickly painted from vapor
a cumulous truth

58 Thinking Outside the Juice Box

What is one little idiosyncrasy about yourself that you usually keep hidden from others? How might revealing it or sharing it with someone make a difference?

One of my favorite things about teaching little kids in our homeschool co-op is seeing their artwork — the details they include, the colors they use, the freedom of the strokes. They are the masters of the outside-the-lines movement, my very favorite type of art.

Recently, observing these little artists looking at their work displayed in our mock-up gallery, I was struck by two things: the awesomeness of their artistry and their *pride* in seeing their work displayed. They love being *visible*.

Trusting Outside the Lines

Being visible is often a big part of the Jump phase. In the Hop and Skip phases, it's fairly easy to remain incognito, hiding your gifts like superhero Underoos. But when you're Jumping...well, eventually, you're probably going to be seen, especially as you start sharing more and more about your particular manifestation with others.

If you've spent a lot of time feeling like an outsider, you may be very sensitive to the comments of others who respond to you, even when they are responding favorably. You might become even *more* aware of not fitting in, especially if you are approaching your manifestation process in a bit of an outside-the-box way and your own version of success looks different from someone else's. It's important to remember that there is no one-size-fits-all pair of superhero Underoos for manifesting; *you get to do this your way.* Remember, everyone who has *ever* done something spectacular has been told, "No, no, that's not how you do it."

Remember the little geniuses who champion the outside-the-lines movement: their freedom, their joy, and their pride in being on display. Borrow a little bit of their pure gusto. You are *allowed* to feel proud. You are allowed to fully claim *your* process, whatever it is, rather than diminish it. Do not share a homeopathic version of yourself, diluted for someone else's safety. Introduce yourself as "*Me*, 100 Percent Pure, Not from Concentrate."

TRY THIS: YOUR NEW LABEL

1. Using crayons or markers, write, "ME, 100 PERCENT PURE, NOT FROM CONCENTRATE" on a piece of paper in big letters.
2. Turn the paper over and write the ingredients that make up the 100 percent nondiluted you. What are the pure, natural ingredients of you?
3. Think of how you can make at least one of your ingredients more visible. How can you let this part of you be seen? Then try another ingredient. Then another. Trust the artistry of your life, in all its glorious outside-the-lines-ness.

HAIKOODLE

play as a scribble
doesn't matter what it means
a world of its own

59 Moving, Stacking, and Nesting Boxes

FUN FACT: In French, a jack-in-the-box is called a *diable en boîte* (literally, "boxed devil").

Think of the most bothersome "little devils" that are causing mischief in your path right now. What happens when you reimagine them as silly tricksters in clown hats, humming "Pop! Goes the Weasel"?

When I was little, I used to crack up at the signs hung up around town that said, "Moving Boxes...Call 555-555-5555." I may not have remembered the phone number right; after all, it was a long time ago. But I *do* remember seeing the signs and imagining boxes that were *actually moving*. I pictured little dancing boxes doing the cancan. Or perhaps marching across the street, with arms and legs. As a result, when I became a parent and learned about the popular baby toy of nesting boxes — those little stacking boxes of decreasing size that go inside one another — I couldn't help but think of animated little boxes setting up house. The image of magical moving boxes still makes me giggle.

A Home for Inner Critics

In the Jump phase, your inner critic can have a field day. We all have many kinds of inner selves; I recommend the amazing work of Hal and Sidra Stone to learn more about how our inner selves sabotage and support us. I definitely have more than a few inner critics, and one of mine lives in *moving boxes* — and not the kind that set up nests or do the cancan.

As I write this book, I am right in the midst of a big move. I am now remembering why moving always appears near the top of those stress indicator lists, even when the move is a good thing, as this particular move is for my family. It actually feels like several moves in one, as we are incorporating boxes (and more boxes) from previous moves that have been in storage for a long time. We have a whole slew of boxes that I haven't opened in decades. I have no idea what is in them. Since they are from another part of my life — a difficult part of my life — I admit they scare me a bit. They are looking me up and down as if I'm the last person picked for the team in gym class. They are mocking me, saying, "*This* is your past, right here — face up to it!"

In the Jump phase, you might find yourself in a strange juxtaposition where time folds upon itself; you are here in the moment taking action, and you are surrounded by boxes holding things from your past. Do you look into these boxes? Or do you move on?

Gaynell's use of a toy metaphor to help her transform an old fear demonstrates the strong hold our past can have on us:

> One of my favorite toys was Careful, the Toppling Tower Game. What is its message for me now? This toy might represent the times I've been in business before, and the other career paths I've followed, that all came toppling down. Its message for me right now is to remember how much fun it is to build the tower, to take the risk in removing the supports, to apply a keen sense of balance.

I can even remember how grandly delighting it is when the tower tumbles and the bell rings out. Everything changes, builds up, falls down. It's in the building and re-creating that the muse and music get made. Best to just move on.

When you are in the Jump phase, you *can't* look back; you can only move on. It is very difficult to look behind you and jump forward. Wait, let me see if I can prove that.... Okay, yes, I just tried, and it is indeed very difficult — and I think I might have pulled a muscle.

The Jump phase is characterized by its purposefulness in direction, the *conscious* way we start at one point and move to another. This requires focus. When memories or thoughts from the past get in the way of our action, we can pack them in boxes and invite them to move away. No old box is getting in the way of *this* Jump!

TRY THIS: MAKE YOUR CRITIC CONTAINER

1. Make a literal container for your inner critic, where it can stay out of your way when necessary and also be called upon when helpful. Pick a box of any size to use for this purpose.

2. Decorate the box with things that would make the inner critic comfortable.

3. Experiment with different ways to close it securely. Does this box need to be stapled, taped, or nailed shut? Do you need a one-way mirror so you can see the critic but it can't see you?

4. Decide what you would like to do with this critic container. Would you like to keep it nearby, to remind you that as you are Jumping, the past can't hurt you? Would you like to decorate the box and transform it into something beautiful? Would you like to hang a sign with your phone number inside the box and see if anyone calls?

Toddlers are encouraged to play with big boxes. Crawling through oversize boxes provides a way to learn spatial awareness and feel comfort and security in cozy, fort-like spaces. Smaller nesting boxes encourage fine motor skills and deduction through trial and error. Playing with boxes of all sizes exercises toddlers' empowerment and imagination. You can play with your critic-container box — it symbolizes the fact that *you can move on*. I know that is what mine is doing for me!

MANIFESTAGRAM
Critics in boxes − Toxic inscribes

HAIKOODLE

play as a big box
marked "Fragile, handle with care"
touch it anyway

TOP TEN STRESSORS FOR TODDLERS

10. Death of a goldfish.
9. Mismanagement of play money.
8. Increased labor hours when playing construction worker.
7. Job change from construction worker to astronaut.
6. Another career change: astronaut to lion tamer.
5. Unemployment rise for lion tamers.
4. Sleep deprivation due to colicky baby doll.
3. Enforced surveillance during sibling interaction.
2. Accident while singing "Wheels on the Bus."
1. Sudden crying outbursts from spilled milk.

60 Turn Your Doubt into a Dare

*If your dream gave you a choice of "truth" or "dare,"
which would you choose, and what would happen next?*

Here's a tool that has the potential to work very quickly to help you tap into action: learn the difference between your *dream* and your *dare*. A dream is something you want to do — like writing a book. A dream may also include results — such as writing a book and getting it published. Or writing a bestseller. Or writing a book and getting it into Ellen DeGeneres's hands, which are probably quite soft from CoverGirl moisturizers.

Your *dare*, on the other hand, is solely based on *your experience*, not outside results. Many people reading this may have a dream to write a book, but each of us will have a different dare. Your dare is an inner positive challenge that is unique to you; *it is designed specifically to counteract your doubts*. When you identify and nurture your dare, it's like suddenly stumbling on a new energy source! See the sidebar for examples of how this works.

EXAMPLES OF TURNING A DOUBT INTO A DARE

A *dare statement* is written specifically to counteract a doubt. Here are four examples:

DOUBT: "I'm worried about what other people think."
DARE: "I dare myself to write a book and tell my truth, and only my truth."

DOUBT: "I just don't think anything I write is good enough."
DARE: "I dare myself to just write a book — not plan or edit, just *write*."

DOUBT: "I get overwhelmed when I think about publication or marketing."
DARE: "I dare myself to write a book and not care at all about publication or marketing until the book is 100 percent written."

DOUBT: "I could never fill a book. It feels too hard; I don't think I could do it."
DARE: "I dare myself to write one paragraph a day.

In the end, your dare statement is something that is more valuable than the outer results of your dream. If you feel a little excited and a little scared when you say your dare, then you know you've landed on the right thing. And that's the truth.

TRY THIS: DOODLE YOUR DARE

1. Write down the biggest doubt you have right now about manifesting your dream. What is the biggest thing that seems to be holding you back?
2. Give yourself a *dare* to counteract the doubt.
3. Double-check your dare statement to make sure that it's not related to external results and that you feel both

excited and scared when you read it. Make adjustments as necessary. This dare is powerful, so playing with it to get it right is time well spent.

4. Draw a playful doodle that represents your dare statement.

ACROWHIM
DARE = Doodle A Revealed Experience

HAIKOODLE

play as truth or dare
telling truths of secret dreams
reveals the true you

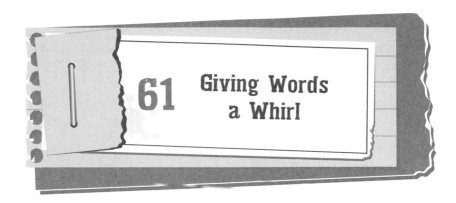

61 Giving Words a Whirl

FUN FACT: The Frisbee was first named the "Whirlo-Way."

Make up a phrase that describes your path as you approach the finish line for your project: the _____ Way.

As someone who wears her wordplay on her sleeve, I am often asked, "Why do you turn everything into wordplay?" There are two reasons: First, it makes me happy, because words are my quickest way to play. It also helps me attract playful people, because those are the folks whom I'd most like to join me in the sandbox. We really can't please everyone all the time, nor should we try. I tell my entrepreneurial clients that if *someone* isn't ridiculing my word-jazz, then it's a good sign I'm not really having fun, which, in turn, means I'm not really attracting the right people.

From the people who *do* enjoy all the word-whimsy — or at least are willing to indulge it — the question I often hear is, "*How* do you come up with all those wild names for things?"

Here's a peek at my play…

My Biggest Wordplay Secret Revealed

So…right now, I am organizing some material for a course I'm writing. It's not feeling playful. I'm not taking action. I'm making a chai latte instead.

I decide to see if I can find a playful portal with words because, as mentioned earlier, words are *my* quickest portal to play.

Organize…hmm…

I will now reveal the very secret, sophisticated way in which I play with words. I go through the alphabet, letter by letter, to find rhymes. There. That's it. *That's* my secret.

So for the word *organize*, I go through the alphabet, and I try each letter on, out loud: *borganize, corganize, dorganize, eorganize, forganize, gorganize, horganize.*…I keep going until I get to *zorganize*. As I move through the list, I note words that might be possibilities.

Then I do the same thing with other syllables. Exploring a rhyme for the second syllable, I find *orcanize*, which reminds me that yes, I *can* do this. For the last syllable, I find *organthighs*, which instantly depresses me and almost sends me for another chai latte, but then I land on *organsighs* — which reminds me that this can be relaxing.

My favorite is *smorgasbordanize*, which might mean laying it all out where there is deliciousness in its variety. Mmm-hmm, that feels good!

Now, with this shift in energy, and with *smorgasbordanize-orcanize-organsighs* in my head, I'm ready to Jump. How about you?

TRY THIS: TRANSWORDATION

1. Write down one word that sums up something you'd like to make more fun.
2. Go through the whole alphabet, in order, adding each letter to the first syllable. Note any words that might inspire you.

3. Do the same thing for the other syllables.

4. Pick one — or more than one — word that gives you a shift in energy.

Ta-da! There's my big secret to quick action!

MANIFESTAGRAM
Play with words, find new meanings =
Find new wily word-paths…sing, "Amen!"

HAIKOODLE
play as lots of words
sleeping in bookshelf bunk beds
dream to be written

62

The Animation of Everyday Objects

FUN FACT: Lionel Trains were invented in 1901 when Joshua Cowen approached a local shop owner with an idea to add movement to display windows as a way to feature whatever product they wanted to display.

What aspects of your dream are ready to be displayed in a window for all to see?

I love the scene in *Mary Poppins* when the kids clean up the nursery and everything in the room comes alive to help. As well as the scene in *The Cat in the Hat* when the cat brings in the Thinga-ma-jigger cleanup machine that helps him "pick up all the things that were down" and he picks up "the cake, and the rake, and the gown." Now, wouldn't you love to be able to snap your fingers and suddenly have the papers organized, the phone calls made, the errands run…and your cake, rake, and gown in their proper places?

Finding Support in Unexpected Places

When you're right smack in the middle of action, at some point, you might be overcome by the thought "Agh! I just can't do this myself!"

Just on the oh-so-very-slight-and-slim chance that you might be able to relate, here is what Dr. Seuss might say:

When feeling this way,
you can play:
use anime
to change the day

Yes, anime, as in *animation*. When you playfully tap into the magic of animation, you can see that you aren't alone, because all around, there are forces that are bigger than you that can help.

For example it helps me, as I sit typing at this computer, to realize:

My Dream is right here with me. Time is with me. Space is giving me a hug. I'm partnering with the computer, and the keyboard delights at my every stroke. The keys are in a friendly competition, saying, "Pick me, pick me," and they all want to join the party. Zxqzxq — that's just a little something for the least-used letters on my keyboard so they don't feel left out. I type these things to realize I am not alone. My Dream is serenading me with love songs. The whole world is vibrating right here with me.

Physics teaches us that every single object has energy. The book in your hands is vibrating. The lamp next to you is vibrating. The clothes on your body are vibrating and alive. You can play with this idea to remember that you are *not* alone, that you are connected with everything.

Look around and see more than what you have seen before. The computer keyboard looks like cobblestones; the computer mouse looks like a waterslide; the thermos looks like a spaceship; the switch on the lamp looks like a tiny domino. Suddenly, your imagination is open again, and so you can get back to the task at hand. The objects are vibrating with you as you see them. Your Dream sings a second chorus of the serenade. You're not doing this alone.

TRY THIS: I SPY WITH MY LITTLE EYE

Try "animating" everyday objects to see them in different ways. Frederick Franck said, "We do a lot of looking: we look through lenses, telescopes, television tubes. Our looking is perfected every day, but we see less and less."

Let your eye fall on something in your immediate environment. *See* it. What else might it look like? What does it remind you of? How does seeing this object in a new, animated way help you connect to the vibration it offers?

You are never alone. Every single object around you is helping you. You've got an energetic team of moving particles doing a kick line in your honor, like the Rockettes at Radio City Music Hall. That's energy. That's movement.

ACROWHIM

ANIMATE = A New Inspiration:
Make Action Transform Ennui

HAIKOODLE

play as a movie
stop-motion animation
captures every laugh

Getting a
Gold Star

FUN FACT: The longest marathon on a pogo stick is 206,864 bounces, achieved by James Roumeliotis in Costa Mesa, California, on July 29, 2011. James bounced for twenty hours and thirteen minutes.

*Each minute you are focused on manifesting your goal,
you are getting closer to achieving it. What might change
if you could view 206,864 minutes as about five months
of itty-bitty jumps getting you closer to your goal?*

If you've spent a lot of time with children who are just learning to speak, you know what it's like to be attached to a funny word pronunciation made by a young child, hoping against hope that the child will *never* learn to say it correctly. One of Kai's first words was "noom" for the word *moon*. I remember being so sad the first time he said it right! Thankfully, another one of our early favorite words has stuck because my family continues to say it all the time: Kai used to pronounce the word *bonus* as "bonust." We now define and use "bonust" as the superlative version of getting a reward when you do something right.

A Little Reward Goes a Long Way

Positive incentives are a great tool for children. A sticker or a certificate or a ribbon feels like gold to a young kid. When Kai was learning to use the toilet, he got a Buzz Lightyear sticker every time he did it right, which thrilled him. It did not, however, thrill my husband, who said it shattered *any* chance of his growing up to work at NASA: "Every time he even *sees* an astronaut, he's going to have to pee!"

In the Jump phase, the goal is action and completion, but sometimes you have to wait a bit to see the *results* of all the actions you are linking together. To help raise your spirits as you wait, you can treat your inner child's sense of pride to some fun rewards.

TRY THIS: COMPLETION CONSTELLATIONS

Go to an office supply or dollar store, and buy a set of gold star stickers. Better yet, buy two sets, because I have the feeling you are going to need them!

Whenever you finish an action — large or small — give yourself a gold star. You can put them anywhere you want: in your calendar, in a journal, on a mirror, on your car dashboard, on your shoes. Create *completion constellations* by adding more and more stars with each action.

With your completion constellations, you get to experience a playful sense of rewarding pride when your actions, in Henry Miller's words, "cluster together like stars." Or, as Buzz Lightyear would say, when your actions take you "to infinity and beyond!"

When you see all those sparkly stars lining up together, the action is undeniable. A deep knowing enters your mind and heart, and you start believing in yourself more and more often — and not just once in a blue "noom."

MANIFESTAGRAM	
Big rewards = Weird brags	

HAIKOODLE
play as blue ribbon
given at the finish line
always comes in first

Feel free
to doodle

64   Summer Camp

FUN FACT: An amazing 64 percent of today's civil, corporate, and political women leaders in the United States were once Girl Scouts.

As you take action toward your goal,
what would you like to "scout out"?
What kinds of information, resources, or assistance do you need?

I went to Girl Scout camp as a child and have lots of summer camp memories. I remember how hot it was under all that horse-riding gear. I remember how camp counselors seemed so old and sophisticated, and now I realize they were probably just in high school. I remember slapping mosquitoes while making those little plastic-type things. What were they called? Aha! Thanks to Google, my memory has been jogged: they were called *lanyards*. It appears that the lanyard is also referred to by other fun names, including *scoubidou* and *boondoggle*. As I read this information, I am left with questions. Did we ever *do* anything with these little plastic crafts? And with a fancy name like *scoubidou* available, why in the world did we call it a *lanyard*?

Lessons from Lanyards

Here are some other things I've learned in my lanyard research: in the summer camp context, lanyards are what they call a "stand-alone craft," where the emphasis is more on the process than the product. The process of intricate weaving has been an arts-and-crafts staple for years, but, apparently, lanyards are actually used today for many purposes, including as name-tags and holders for valuables such as cameras, cell phones, and USB flash drives. At the rate today's technology is rolling out these gadgets, I imagine we're keeping the Girl Scouts pretty busy. In many cases, a lanyard keeps a valuable item not only connected to its owner, but also in plain sight. Just as lanyards help us keep an eye on things we don't want to lose, keeping important things in plain sight is an important part of the Jump phase.

TRY THIS: YOUR CRAFTY CONNECTION TOOL

1. Imagine you could have a lanyard — or a scoubidou or boondoggle, if you prefer — that could instantly connect you to whatever you most need to keep in plain sight right now. What do you need to stay connected to, in order to ensure its visibility at all times?

2. What aspects of yourself do you fear losing? What would you like to keep readily on display?

3. Draw a quick sketch of your special connectivity tool. How might life be different if you could create it and put it to use?

ACROWHIM
CAMP = Childlike Artistry Modeling Play

HAIKOODLE
play as a campfire
hearing all our old stories
sparks fly and tell s'more

TOP TEN SIGNS YOU WERE A GIRL SCOUT

10. Whenever cookies are served, you find yourself overcome with the urge to *sell* them.

9. When a child indicates his or her age with three fingers, you burst into the Girl Scout Promise.

8. You refuse to eat trail mix while not in the act of hiking.

7. You think that green scarf would look great as a sash!

6. When completing a report at work, you look around to see where your badge is.

5. You still remember that one badge you could never finish, and continually overcompensate in this area.

4. Speaking of badges, you have a distinct opinion about the "new badges" and the "old badges" and could easily prove your point in a debate.

3. When you make a new female friend, you find yourself wondering, "Hmm...is she silver or gold?"

2. You associate the word *thin* with *mints*.

1. When someone says they brought brownies, you look around for the little girls.

65 Cuckoo Clocks

FUN FACT: It is believed that the cuckoo clock was inspired by the sound from the wind bellows of a church organ, which was reproduced in a small form in the clock, creating two different notes that resemble the sound of a bird.

What would you like to tell time?
How would like to ask time to assist you right now?

When it comes to productivity, most traditional approaches will focus on *management*: managing your time, your day, your tasks, your finances. When I wrote *Creating Time*, I was very clear that I didn't want to write a time-management book; I wanted to write a *time re-imaginement* book. Whenever we say we want to manage or master time, it automatically sets up an image of a dramatic battle: "It's me against time!" So I wanted to write a different kind of book about time, to help us reinvent our relationship with the clock and create more time by activating more creativity.

You Hold the Power to Create Time

Your beliefs about time, like anything else, create your realities about time. Whatever you say about time is true. That is really important in the Jump phase, so I'll say it again: *whatever you say about time is true.* (Cue the cuckoo clock sound…)

Well, it might sound cuckoo, but it's true: you create your own experience of time. You create time with your beliefs and choices. You create time with every thought about time that enters your head or leaves your lips. If you are trying to fight, chase, manage, master, or — God forbid — *kill* time, how do you think time will treat you in return? Instead of yelling at it, screaming at it, saying, "There's not enough of you!" what if you could befriend it, dance with it, *partner* with it, instead? What if time could be your ally, your buddy, you collaborator, your bff? Changing the way you operate in time starts by changing your relationship with time itself.

Time is not just hours; time is *ours*. Grab it by the hand, apologize for all those times you've hurt its feelings, and invite time to Jump through the sprinkler with you and get soaked to the skin.

TRY THIS: DESIGN A NEW WATCH

With today's gadgety phones, wearing a watch is becoming less common, but if you *did* wear a watch, and could design a watch that had *any* image on it, what would you most want to see whenever you checked the time? See the sidebar for some examples.

Get your crayons, and draw a picture of what this watch looks like. How would your life be different if you saw this image whenever you checked the time?

MANIFESTAGRAM
Telling time = Gentle limit

HAIKOODLE

play as a small clock
the alarm is set for now
wake up to your life

66 Shake, Rattle, Roll, Repeat

FUN FACT: In the Middle Ages, parents gave their children silver baby rattles as a playful way to offer protection from the plague, as silver was known to fight illness.

How might your current action plan
benefit from being shaken up and rattled a bit?

One of the challenges of the Jump phase is that there is generally a lot of repetition, as Jumping is often about repetition and pattern. This can be difficult, especially for people who are most comfortable when Skipping. Jumping means continuing to do the same thing, again and again, over and over. Jumping is often about repetition and pattern. *Jumping is often about repetition and pattern.* **Jumping is often about repetition and pattern.** Did I mention that Jumping is often about repetition and pattern? It may not sound like fun, but it's also not as hard as it seems when you appreciate its purpose.

The Value of Repetition and Pattern

Repetition welcomes momentum in our bodies and establishes neural pathways that support action. In the Jump phase, you can have fun creating *new* associations between play, action, and productivity, much like a baby experiments with a rattle. A baby's inner monologue may sound something like "Ga ga goo ba bab dgah bobble," which, loosely translated, is "That looks fun. I'll shake it. Cool, something happens. I'll try it again."

This is what *productivity* is, too:

1. That looks fun!
2. I'll do something.
3. I notice something happens.
4. I'll do it again.

Marva tells a remarkable story about when she had planned to do a series of talks in her local community center but nobody had signed up. She told her mentor, "I guess that means I'll cancel," but he set her straight! He told her she needed to show up every single week, set up the chairs, make the coffee, and sit there by herself for the full hour. Then she needed to clean up the coffee pot, put away the chairs, turn off the lights, go home, and come back the next week and do the same thing. He told her she needed to show up for herself.

So she did this every week. Over time, people started trickling in. When they did, she welcomed them to sit in the usually empty chairs. Each week, more and more people came. By the end of the series, it was standing-room only. Through tapping into repetition and regularity, she found momentum, and momentum found her.

TRY THIS: YOUR DAILY PLAY LOG

1. Write the following phrase (including the blank line) on a piece of paper seven times, with a bit of space in between each phrase: "Today I will play as I complete _____."

2. Go ahead and complete the first phrase with the first thing that comes to mind — for example, "Today I will play as I complete a phone call to a prospective client."

3. Congratulations! You have created a daily log for your-

self for the coming week, and you've already begun the practice of using it. Put this sheet somewhere where you will see it every morning. Complete that same phrase every day for seven days; show up for yourself through pattern and repetition. This is your *playful productivity hygiene*, which is as important as brushing your teeth.

ACROWHIM
REPEAT = Reality Evolves, People Echo: A Triumph

HAIKOODLE

play as a rattle
a baby's hand holds it tight
engraved memories

67 Jumping Water

FUN FACT: The world's first recognizable fire sprinkler system was installed in the Theatre Royal, Drury Lane, in London in 1812.

What "fire" would you like to put out right now?
What might you imagine sprinkling over this situation
to extinguish the negativity?

It's no secret that toys and play have changed a lot, especially since the advent of the computer. In this day and age, in which toys and games have become increasingly sophisticated, I was so happy to be at a kid's birthday party recently and see that children still love running back and forth through a simple, old-fashioned lawn sprinkler. There was a part of me that sighed and thought that perhaps these pint-size leaders of our future were going to be okay after all.

Water Play

Water is such a great conduit for play. Many babies experience their first play experience with their bath toys. Water is used in play therapy to aid relaxation in kids recovering from trauma. Swimming pools and oceans lend themselves to frolicking. Many adults' favorite ways to play — boating, fishing, swimming, and surfing — involve water.

Water is also a great metaphor for *movement*. Water finds a way to go where it needs to go. It will find a channel and flow to it. It is the source of all life. *Water is like action.*

When Kai was first learning to combine words, he called fountains "jumping water." No matter the format — from a decorative fountain in a fancy shopping mall to a simple water fountain outside the restrooms — they were all "jumping water." Just like fountains, your action during the Jumping phase can look like a lot of different things, too. Action can look slow, graceful, and steady. It can look grandiose, like the fountains at the Bellagio in Las Vegas. It can be a subtle decorative element or the centerpiece of an environment. It can be something to admire or something with which to interact.

What kind of water play will be most helpful to you as you Jump?

Donna was stuck when it came to taking action. She said she felt like she was being swallowed up, as if she had been carried out to sea in the rough ocean waves. When we played with the water metaphor a bit, she identified the fact that she loves the shallow beaches of Hawaii, which feel so different from the turbulent waters off the California coast. Donna transformed a small business into her "shallow beach," and picking the right metaphor made all the difference in her ability to take action.

> ## TRY THIS: BODIES OF WORK AND WATER

1. Take a piece of paper and your crayons, and draw a body of water that symbolizes how you feel right now, in the middle of your Jump phase; leave some free space on the page for another drawing. What is the size, shape, and form of this body of water? What about it feels good, and what about it feels difficult? Are you surfing on rough waters? Are you paddling in a too-small canoe? Are you

at the beach but still not in the water? Just draw whatever image comes to mind.

2. On another part of the page, draw a body of water that represents the experience you imagine having once you have manifested your intention. What kind of water represents this experience? What is your ideal destination, symbolized by water?

3. Draw a connector of some kind between the two bodies of water, such as a path, a bridge, a ladder, a river, or a pier. Again, whatever comes out of your crayon is just perfect.

4. On or around this connector, write steps that will help your water current get from your current water to your future water. What do you notice?

MANIFESTAGRAM
Water play = La! We party!

HAIKOODLE

play as a fountain
flow, fun, family, and free
drinking in your youth

TIME TO DOODLE

68   Playing with Piggy Banks

What is in your metaphorical piggy bank besides money? In what other ways, besides money, are your current actions "paying off"?

Though you may not be focused on earning money through your dream, I imagine you are looking for some kind of *return* on the investment you are making in your manifesting process. Whatever result you are seeking as you manifest — be it money or something else you want to receive — you can play with the way these results show up and how you experience them.

Playful Prosperity

Years ago, during a time when my financial situation felt bleak, I decided that I needed to be focusing on something besides my empty bank account. I invented a new kind of playful accounting system where I recorded all the things for which I was grateful in an old accounting ledger as a way to recognize that prosperity and abundance come in many forms. It was amazing how prosperous

I felt as my daily "balance" of blessings kept getting bigger and bigger. Sure enough, before long, my outward financial picture started changing as well. I believed in this system so much that I created an online program called "Accounting Your Blessings" to inspire others to try it, too.

This process made me realize that wealth, like anything, is truly perception, and that by simply analyzing prosperity through a different measurement system — in this case, through gratitude — we can make remarkable changes.

TRY THIS: ACCOUNTING YOUR BLESSINGS

Create a financial tracking system to keep track of your blessings. You can use a checkbook record, spreadsheet, ledger book, or accounting app. In whatever system you choose, keep track of your blessings by assigning a "prosperity value" to each blessing on a scale from one to ten (for example, an unexpected client referral might be an eight, a nice flower on the side of the road a four, and so on).

At the end of each week, do the books and experience your "balance" getting bigger and bigger! This is an excellent way to cultivate a regular gratitude practice while creating a sense of "muscle memory" for wealth.

ACROWHIM
BALANCE = Bending And Leaning
And Not Collapsing Energy

HAIKOODLE

play as abundance
counted beans become huge stalks
magic in the sky

69 A Play List for Productivity

FUN FACT: Gumby wasn't originally meant as a toy; it was created as a character for an animated jazz video.

The Gumby toy is known for its flexible construction. In what way might you "jazz up" your current routine to be a bit more flexible and playful?

ony knows the best way to get on my good side is to turn a moment into a musical, just as I know the best way to get on his good side is to give him a complex math problem to calculate. Though I haven't done much singing in many years, musical theater still is embedded deep in my soul. After all, I grew up on Rodgers and Hammerstein LPs, attended a performing arts high school, and spent my early twenties pursuing a theater career in New York City. So the idea that life could turn into a musical — where anyone can burst into song at any moment — makes me quite happy.

Playing Music

I remember one time when my family returned home after a vacation, we were greeted by an *awful* smell coming from the kitchen. A big bin of food from the refrigerator had been left out in our absence, and needless to say, it was not pleasant. Tony, bless him, turned the moment into a musical and began rewriting the lyrics to "Margaritaville" and other popular tunes. I imagine this is what Robert Henri meant when he said, "Your whole heart is in the singing." The scent of our laughter deodorized that whole house! And in case you are interested, surprisingly few words rhyme with *fridge*.

Whether you sing a song with new lyrics or introduce a sound track to play in the background of your life, music helps you Jump! When music is playing, everything changes. I'll never forget the first time I experienced tuning forks applied as a healing tool, during an acupuncture session. The best way I can describe it is to say that the *air* changed when the tuning forks were chimed. Much research has been done on the effect of sound, specifically musical sound, on our health. When you sing, or even hum, you are changing the molecules in the space around you.

TRY THIS: YOUR MANIFESTATION MIX TAPE

It's time to romance your project with music, like a sentimental mix tape. When you work and play on your project, what kind of music is most inspiring? Does your project like classical music? Country? Opera? Jazz? Old show tunes? Does it like to get up and dance?

Experiment with new music styles to see if they bring about interesting changes in your creativity. It takes so little effort to romance with music when working; you just need to create a little time to set up your playlist...so you can play!

MANIFESTAGRAM
Play music = Yup, I's calm!

HAIKOODLE

play as symphony
strings, theory, cacophony
knowing it's in tune

TOP TEN SONGS TO INSPIRE PRODUCTIVITY

Classical music promotes focus; ambient music encourages flow; but inspiring lyrics work best for me. I love hearing a motivating message expressed through song. Here are a few I like to use when I need a kick start:

10. "I Was Here" by Beyoncé
 9. "Eye of the Tiger" by Survivor
 8. "Dreams" by the Cranberries
 7. "Don't Stop Me Now" by Queen
 6. "Girl on Fire" by Alicia Keys
 5. "Unwritten" by Natasha Bedingfield
 4. "Stronger (What Doesn't Kill You)" by Kelly Clarkson
 3. "Don't Stop Believin'" by Journey
 2. "Do It Anyway" by Martina McBride
 1. The theme song from *Rocky*

70
If You're Happy and You Know It...

What sounds like more fun than a barrel of monkeys to you? How can you bring more of that spirit into a mundane, boring task?

There are a lot of playful toys and tools in the world that are related to monkeys: retro Sea-Monkeys, monkey bars, monkeys jumping on the bed, sock monkeys, flying monkeys, barrels of monkeys, and, of course, that strange little chimp with the clapping cymbals.

When I was a child, one of my dad's favorite phrases was "Stop that monkey business!" I wonder, what kind of *business* would a monkey run? Somewhere there's a joke in there, perhaps involving the words *ape* and *proprietorship* and maybe *bananas*, but it's not coming to me right now. If you happen to figure it out, please break it to me gently.

The Importance of Equalizing Actions

When I play, sometimes it works, and sometimes it doesn't, as evidenced by the earnest but unsuccessful effort at wit in the previous paragraph. Part of Jumping is being okay when things *don't* all go well. In the Jump phase, you get to use play to *equalize all actions so that they all are important.* You can plug into positive, playful energy no matter what action you are doing.

Walt Whitman's *Specimen Days* is a collection of journal entries in which three key characters express the energy of life across a spectrum of events, both banal and extraordinary, glorious and horrific. Whitman encourages us to see that every single moment is a specimen of life.

In a meaningful life, washing dishes is no less sacred than giving birth. Painting a single stroke is no less magnificent than completing a grand-scale masterpiece. A failed joke is as playful as crisp wit.

Somehow, it is all *life*, and one moment is not more "lifely" than the other. The hard part, of course, is to remember this sense of grace, constancy, and unity in our day-to-day lives, and to give every action attention and even applause.

TRY THIS: CLAP YOUR HANDS

1. Get two paper plates, or cut two large circles out of sturdy paper.

2. On one of your circles, write down something really amazing that you have achieved during your manifestation process — a powerful moment where everything felt just right and you knew, in that lovely snapshot in time, that your dreams really *were* coming true.

3. On another circle, write down something ridiculously wrong that has happened along the way — something that really felt like a failure, misstep, or irreversible challenge…the kind of moment where you knew, in that dreadful splotch in time, that everything you were trying to do was completely hopeless.

4. These two circles are symbols for cymbals. Take them and clap them together, like the little clapping chimp (no need to bare your teeth, unless you want to). Give your-

self some hearty applause for *both* of these moments and every single moment in between. You deserve applause for all of it.

5. Extra credit: Try to say "symbols for cymbals" five times fast. Remember, mastering the tongue twister is no more successful than mucking it up. Either way, take a bow.

ACROWHIM
APPLAUSE = A Powerful Place:
Lauding An Unexciting Specimen Enthusiastically

HAIKOODLE

play as percussion
hi-hat, drum, and xylophone
cymbals improvised

71 Curly Ribbons and Finish Lines

FUN FACT: The Boston Marathon's yellow-and-blue finish line is an icon to avid runners, but the actual site of the finish line has changed four times since the first marathon — then known as the American Marathon — in 1897.

*How might you give your project some room
to move and change a bit, even as you near the finish line?*

My son, Kai, has seen several scenes in *Chariots of Fire*, and, as he will thoughtfully explain, "You know, a chariot is really a cart. And it's not really on fire — that's just a *symbol*." He seems to have a special connection with the film, especially the story of Eric Liddell, whose athletic gift comes from the faith in his heart.

Leading with Your Heart

Kai has a metabolic disorder that affects his bone structure and growth, and with his physical differences, he probably will not grow up to be a runner. Yet he's finding his own way to feel comfortable in his body, even in playing sports. For the past year, he's been part of a local wrestling team, and he loves every moment of this. His coach, Melvin — a strong man with a soft heart of gold who is truly gifted at keeping things playful for the little kids — once told Tony, "He's got what I can't teach — he's got heart." Kai already knows that his heart can take his body anywhere he wants to go. For him, and those of us lucky enough to watch, that *is* crossing the finish line.

What about you? How might your *heart* help you get to that finish line? How might your heart help you know that you are closer than you've ever been?

TRY THIS: MAKING YOUR FINISH LINE

1. Buy a spool of ribbon (rope or yarn will work, too, but spaghetti will not).
2. Pick a corner in your home and extend the ribbon from wall to wall, like a finish line.
3. Add these words to your ribbon: "You have never been closer."
4. Every time you look at it, you will be reminded that you are so very close and you just need to keep leading with your heart!

MANIFESTAGRAM
The finish line = Shh…feelin' in it.

HAIKOODLE

play as the applause
thunderstorm of approval
starts with my heartbeat

72 Service Soap Bubbles

FUN FACT: In 1948, Candy Land was invented by Eleanor Abbott as an escape for kids in the polio ward in a San Diego hospital.

What is a cause that is important to you?
What group of people are you most naturally driven to help?

As discussed in the previous chapter, completion energy means pulling in to the finish line. Sometimes the very end of the project is the hardest. We need to get that *last wind* to help us get there. My favorite way to pick up a bit of wind as I'm nearing the end of a project is to connect to the power of *service*.

Miracles as Accelerators

When you feel like you are at the end of your rope, it's easy to throw up your hands and say, "I need a miracle." Another choice is to say, "I need to *give* a miracle." This is what it means to plug into service. *Giving a miracle* is the greatest Jump accelerator I know.

The initial idea for *Artella* magazine came when I was reading about what Deepak Chopra calls the "Law of Giving," which is this: what you want for yourself, give to another. At the time I read it, what I wanted most was to have my art and writing published. Within Chopra's words, I saw something different — that I could help *others* publish their art and writing. This led to self-publishing a magazine, which began a path I could never have predicted. Because of this experience, I return to the Law of Giving whenever I need a bit of acceleration.

Service can refer to many things. You can give a miracle in a very small, simple way. Service does *not* mean giving *everything* away or sharing in a way that depletes you. There also is a time and place for everything, and it's not always the time for service. When someone is hit by a bus, you don't walk up to her on the street as she lies there and say, "I know you are a bit preoccupied with the sirens and stretcher and bandages right now, but you know what you really need? A great big dose of helping somebody *else* right now!" Service is nothing you *should* do. You should never enter into an act of service because someone else has told you to do it, like in a game of Simon Says. Service comes from within you and your heart.

When you are being of service, you plug back into the greatest purpose in life. Nothing feels better. Nothing is more magical.

TRY THIS: SENSES OF SERVICE

Grab your crayons and complete this poem, writing each line in a different color:

Service looks like _____
Service smells like _____
Service feels like _____
Service tastes like _____

What do you see in the poem you just wrote? What insights or ideas are revealed about the role that service might play?

If you want to try out my favorite Jump accelerator, here are some questions to help you tap into the spirit of service:

• What needs and causes really touch you deeply?
• Whom do you really wish you could help?

- What is something you want for yourself? How might you give that very thing to someone else?

ACROWHIM
SERVICE = Seeing Everything Revolve:
Vitality In Constant Energy

HAIKOODLE

play as giving back
wrapping up a ribboned gift
sending it express

73 Playing with Dominoes

As you are immersed in action, what is one personal record that you would like to match or beat?

ause and effect is a philosophical concept observed in just about every aspect of our lives. However, it can be very discouraging to connect every single action to an expected result. Instead of cause and effect, we can play with the *domino* effect, in which a small change causes a similar change nearby, which then causes another similar change, and so on.

The Domino Effect

Before I started Artella, I tried many different creative projects. Typical to my Jump nature, I'd make things happen very quickly, but I would also give up when things didn't work out. When I didn't get the results I wanted, I'd think, "Well, it just wasn't meant to be," since I thought I was supposed to follow the signals I was getting on the outside. What I really needed to do, however, was follow the messages on the *inside*. It was when I aligned with what I was *feeling* — rather than what I was experiencing as a result — that I found myself able to sustain my momentum all the way through one completion after another.

Imagine this scenario: When Lorie posts a flyer about an upcoming workshop in a health food store, she is expecting a certain number of people to see the flyer and hoping for a certain number of people to register for the workshop as a result. If she exceeds the expected number of registrations, then she's totally *elated*. If she doesn't reach it, she's totally *deflated*. Where is the balance?

Now consider a new scenario: When she posts the flyers, what she is *really* doing is expressing her intent to share her passion everywhere she is drawn to do so. She does the same when she strikes up a conversation with a stranger at the coffee shop; when she asks a friend to hand out some coupons for the workshop in his church group; when she takes out an ad in the local paper; and when she writes a meaningful article in a local magazine that mentions the upcoming workshop. She still wants to attract people to her workshop, but she is putting her focus on the *collective* of authentic actions rather than on expectations related to a particular result. The results of her actions don't occur in a straight, linear fashion, but move in spirals and unexpected swirls.

Take a look at these options. Which feels more motivating for you?

"This week I will book five new coaching clients."
"This week I will bring up coaching in five new conversations."

Of course these are not mutually exclusive — it's not one or the other — but you will probably have a stronger connection with one of the options. *Which one feels like it taps into your momentum?* That's the one to help you Jump!

Do an online search for "dominoes in a spiral video" to find videos of dominoes toppling in a spiral. As you enjoy the hypnotic experience of watching these amazing creations, imagine all of the actions *you* take — big or small — becoming one entity moving in a slow spiral rather than a predictable, linear sequence. How might this concept help you detach from specific results in your next actions and feel the collective movement of everything working together?

MANIFESTAGRAM
No cause and effect = Effect on us: a dance

HAIKOODLE

play as a ripple
a legacy unaware
touches the whole pond

74 Leaving Some of Your Toys Behind

FUN FACT: In the world of Strawberry Shortcake, the toy makers decided to rename Raspberry Tart because they thought with that name, she'd get "a reputation." She became Raspberry Torte instead.

Imagine that "surrender" is a delicious dessert or pastry.
What does it taste like?

I bawled my eyes out during *Toy Story 3*. I mean, like sobbing, heaving, Lifetime-movie-type tears. Seeing Andy reconnect with the toys from his childhood just opened the floodgates of emotion. I'm not alone; my friends have had similar experiences, and I've even seen it included in lists of movie tearjerkers.

Surrendering Mid-Jump

As you grow and change, you *will* leave things behind. Sometimes they are important things that you've held on to for a long time, like a childhood security toy. You leave behind old identities. You leave behind beliefs, labels, relationships, and sometimes even your deepest dreams. You shed skin and surrender to become what you are to become.

Manifesting a dream means giving up who you think you are.

You must want your dream more than you want the safety net of your old stories. You must leave behind the parts of you and your life that do not align with what you are creating.

Throughout the manifestation process, fears come up in different ways:

- In the Hop phase, when fears come up, you can allow yourself to process the feelings, dig deeper, and get to the bottom of them. This is all part of your preparation for what is to come. On one of her beautiful greeting card designs, my friend terri st. cloud says, "It is not enough to find your passion — you must dive straight into the fire of your fear, where you can grab it and hold it until it transforms you."

- In the Skip phase, when fears come up, your best choice is to simply move in a different direction. Follow the energy, and look for what feels sparkly.

- In the Jump phase, your best action is to transform fears *quickly*. "Get in and get out" is what I say to my clients.

Jumping is *not* the time for comprehensive analysis and processing. I'm not saying to deny your emotions — but remember, in the full manifestation process, everything has its time. If you are truly committed to Jumping, diving deeply into a fear isn't going to sustain you. You can't jump up in the air and then decide you don't want to; you have to trust, surrender, and allow yourself to land.

TRY THIS: JUMPING IN THE LEAVES

It's time to leave something behind, and you can use *leaves* to play with this idea. This activity invites you to play with nature, where you'll naturally connect with the cyclical energy of release and regrowth.

1. Go on a walk and gather leaves. If you like, you can bring your crayons and some paper and do some simple crayon rubbings; simply place a leaf underneath a piece

of paper, and color on the paper. The leaf's shape and subtleties will come through in your colorful rubbing.

2. Look closely at each leaf. What does it remind you of — its color, shape, size? How might the leaf represent something from your life that you are ready to leave behind?

3. Create something to mark the occasion of this surrender. You might make something out of your leaves or write a short poem about your experience, as I've included below.

LEAVING BEHIND

What looked like a walk
to beyond or nearer
was a dive into red-gold
out of silked soiled darkness
feeling muscles long cold
in my head and bones
and in my longing
to see more
than what a thing is
and leave it all behind

ACROWHIM
LEAVING = Letting Every Attachment Vanish
In Nascent Growth

HAIKOODLE

play as a small prayer
"Thank you for the finger paint"
my wet canvas smiles

FUN FACT: The game of backgammon, which has existed in one form or another for several millennia, dates back to ancient Egypt.

As you think back on your playful manifestation experience, what is one thing you'd like to do differently next time? What would you like to include in the "next version" of your manifesting game?

I am looking out the window of my new office, in the home we just moved into a few weeks ago. I am admiring the spring wildflowers bursting from the ground. It's extra fun because they are completely surprising — we moved into this house in winter, when the branches were bare and the ground was unadorned. Now patches of brightly colored blossoms are filling the property with color, like a Parcheesi game board made of flowers. Every day, a new colorful surprise is outside the window.

The Ways Nature Plays

I am reflecting on the play of nature. Leaves go Technicolor for fall; for winter, the air starts to smell like white Popsicles as the geese squawk toward their southern pilgrimage; the daffodils and tiger lilies bloom by the side of the road to signal spring; the fields of country sunflowers stand tall at the beginning of summer.

Of course, these symbols change from place to place. In warmer climates, the coming of the winter season may have nothing to do with chilly air and snow angels but might be signified by happy-jagged rows of cutout children's hands colored green to look like holly. Everywhere, we have symbols that we associate with the turning of seasons and cycles.

Elisabeth Kübler-Ross said, "How do geese know when to fly to the sun? Who tells them the seasons? How do we, humans, know when it is time to move on? As with migrant birds, so surely with us, there is a voice within, if only we would listen to it, that tells us so certainly when to go forth into the unknown."

In the manifestation process, there are also signs and symbols that can show us that a new cycle of creativity is ending or beginning. Just as the geese feel the chilly air to know it is time to fly south, there are signals that let us know when it is time to move on from a project or hibernate after its completion. As summer sunflowers must die before they bloom again, our creative fire must become dim from time to time so that it can return and shine in a way that sustains and supports the spreading of seeds in the wind.

TRY THIS: YOUR GAME OF LIFE

1. Imagine that the manifestation journey you've taken is a board game. What is it called? How is it played? What do you use for the playing piece that you move around the board?

2. Grab your crayons and make a simple sketch of what the board looks like. Let yourself have some fun with this. Add a few places that you want to "land" as you continue to play.

3. You are likely familiar with the Game of Life, the popular board game. But what does it mean for you to play the game of life, of *your* life? How does it feel to bring the

game out of your head and fully manifest your inklings in tangible ink while allowing others to play, too? And… what happens next in your game?

> MANIFESTAGRAM
> Keep playing = Apply ink. Gee!

HAIKOODLE

play as hop, skip, jump
closer than we think it is
just a choice away

Congratulations — you've made it around.
It's time to pass Go. Collect two hundred dollars.
Keep playing.

{ Don't forget to doodle }

Acknowledgments

Manifestagrams of thanks go to:

Arthiss Kliever = I serve this lark.
Carmen Taggart = REM: ACT art gang
Dan Gremminger = Grin-merged man
Georgia Hughes = Gosh, I agree. Hug!
Jean E. Sides = I sense jade.
Jill Allison Bryan = I'll join bran's ally.
Jill Badonsky = Jolly ink dabs
Julia Briggs = Rib-jig gal: us
Launa Kliever = Aura-level kin
Lonnie Dean Kliever = Old knee; inner alive
Marc Allen = Learn calm.
Paula Swenson = Saw no sun....Leap!
Susan Kennedy (SARK) = Sky near naked suns
Tama J. Kieves = Ask. Met. A jive.
Terry Jordan = An err-dry jot.

In addition, I thank these frolicsome folks who made this book possible:

The entire Artella team, who make work feel like play every single day! For significant contributions to this book, I owe a

special thank-you to Radio Flyer Robin OK for all her research romp, Lite-Brite Liz Gow for her terrific transcriptions, and Imaginarium Irina Naskinova for her technical tenacity.

Everyone who has traveled through Artella Land, especially the ARTbundance community and MMM manifestors. I am so very lucky to have students and clients who are such inspiring playmates. And I give a brand-new box of crisp crayons to all who gave permission to quote their stories in this book.

The awesome team at New World Library: Kristen Cashman, Tracy Cunningham, Tona Pearce Myers, Kim Corbin, Munro Magruder, and Jonathan Wichmann. I am also deeply appreciative of Mark Colucci, who provided excellent copyediting with a sense of humor.

All the parents and kids at Common Ground Homeschool co-op, who surround our family with both play and purpose.

Dallas Children's Theatre, for two generations of play.

Wordsmith.org's Internet Anagram Server, my new favorite tech toy.

My extended family, friends, and angels from all corners of life who have kept playing with me in both happy and hard times. Hopping, Skipping, and Jumping sometimes means falling down; thanks for all the times you have helped me get back up.

Lastly, my deepest gratitude to:

Anthony Makridakis = Oh, kind karma sanity
Kai Yanni Makridakis = A kid-kin, sky-air mania

You two are my playfully manifest *and* my meaningful life.

Notes

Page 4 *Rapid eye movement (REM) sleep*: Stuart Brown, *Play: How It Shapes the Brain, Opens the Imagination, and Invigorates the Soul* (New York: Avery, 2009), 41.

Page 4 *study of homicidal young men*: "Play Deprived Life — Devastating Result," National Institute for Play, accessed June 23, 2014, www.nifplay.org/vision/early-study/.

Page 4 *play might provide a model*: Anthony D. Pellegrini, Danielle Dupuis, and Peter K. Smith, "Play in Evolution and Development," *Developmental Review* 27, no. 2 (2007): 261–76, http://evolution.bing hamton.edu/evos/wp-content/uploads/2008/11/Pellegrini01.pdf.

Page 4 *Play behaviors of both animals*: Bob Hughes, *Evolutionary Playwork*, 2nd ed. (New York: Routledge, 2012), 49.

Page 5 *Studies of play in various countries*: Jaipaul L. Roopnarine, "Cultural Variations in Beliefs about Play, Parent-Child Play, and Children's Play: Meaning for Childhood Development," in *The Oxford Handbook of the Development of Play*, ed. Peter Nathan and Anthony D. Pellegrini, September 2012, www.oxfordhandbooks.com/view /10.1093/oxfordhb/9780195393002.001.0001/oxfordhb-9780195393002 -e-003.

Page 5 *When children's recess time*: Romina M. Barros, Ellen J. Silver, and Ruth E. K. Stein, "School Recess and Group Classroom Behavior," *Pediatrics* 123, no. 2 (2009): 431–36, http://pediatrics.aappublications. org/content/123/2/431.full.

Page 5 *The inclination to "play pretend"*: Rachel E. White, *The Power of Play: A Research Summary on Play and Learning* (St. Paul: Minnesota Children's Museum, n.d.), 15–23, accessed June 23, 2014, www.mcm.org/uploads/MCMResearchSummary.pdf.

Page 5   *the rise in obesity*: Nick Ng, "Obesity in Childhood Could Be Solved with More Play," *Guardian Liberty Voice*, March 21, 2014, http://guardianlv.com/2014/03/obesity-in-childhood-could-be-solved -with-more-play/.

Page 5   *time children spend playing*: Dorothy G. Singer et al., "Children's Pastimes and Play in Sixteen Nations: Is Free-Play Declining?," *American Journal of Play* 1 (Winter 2009): 283–312.

Page 23   *According to Hasbro*: "Play-Doh Brand Modeling Compound Makes a 'Scent-Sational' Debut as It Celebrates 50 Years," Business Wire, May 1, 2006, www.businesswire.com/news/home/2006050100 5660/en/Play-Doh-Brand-Modeling-Compound-Scent-Sational -Debut-Celebrates.

Page 27   *Lego's name*: Tine Froberg Mortensen, "LEGO History Timeline," The LEGO Group, January 9, 2012, http://aboutus.lego.com/en-us /lego-group/the_lego_history.

Page 30   *The phrase "Happy Birthday"*: Roger Drukker, "Birthday Cake History," Articles on the Web, June 1, 2007, www.articles-on-the-web .com/hobbies/birthday-cake-history-105616.html.

Page 33   *The yo-yo is believed to be*: "Fascinating Facts about the Invention of the Yo-Yo by Donald F. Duncan in 1928," The Great Idea Finder, last modified March 2005, www.ideafinder.com/history/inventions/yoyo.htm.

Page 37   *It takes eighty feet*: Mary Bellis, "History of the Slinky Toy," About.com, accessed May 1, 2014, http://inventors.about.com/od /sstartinventions/a/slinky.htm.

Page 40   *Thomas Edwin Stevens*: Sasha Archibald, David Serlin, and William L. Bird Jr., "By the Numbers: An Interview with William L. Bird, Jr.," *Cabinet*, Fall 2004, www.cabinetmagazine.org/issues/15 /paintbynumbers.php.

Page 42   *A typical child*: Tim Walsh, *Timeless Toys: Classic Toys and the Playmakers Who Created Them* (Kansas City, MO: Andrews McMeel, 2005), 20.

Page 44   *The "alphabet song"*: "The Alphabet Song — Where Did It Come From?," Kidsongs, accessed May 1, 2014, www.kidsongs.com/page /ABCSongHistory/.

Page 45   *"The object is not"*: Margery Ryerson, comp., *The Art Spirit, by Robert Henri: Notes, Articles, Fragments of Letters and Talks to Students, Bearing on the Concept and Technique of Picture Making, the Study of Art Generally, and on Appreciation* (Philadelphia: Lippincott, 1923), 118.

Page 47   *play for autistic children*: Shirley S. Wang, "Targeting Child's Play to Help Tackle Autism," *Wall Street Journal*, May 9, 2012, http://online .wsj.com/news/articles/SB10001424052702304151104577389893715036310.

Page 50   *Each standard Monopoly game*: "12 More Interesting Facts about

Money — Part 2," Delray Credit Counseling, accessed May 1, 2014, www.delraycc.com/InterestingMoney/12MoreAmazingMoneyFacts /tabid/183/Default.aspx.

Page 50 *more Monopoly money printed*: Ibid.

Page 53 *Samuel Allen invented*: Walsh, *Timeless Toys*, 4.

Page 54 *"When it is going well"*: Brown, *Play*, 138.

Page 56 *a song about two enemies:* "In Praise of the Children," Parlor Songs Academy, July 2003, www.parlorsongs.com/issues/2003-7/thismonth /feature.php.

Page 56 *the subject of a plagiarism lawsuit*: "Playmates (Song)," last modified February 7, 2014, http://en.wikipedia.org/wiki/Playmates_(song).

Page 57 *various kinds of social play*: "Subsets of Social Play," National Institute for Play, accessed May 1, 2014, www.nifplay.org/social_play _subsets.html.

Page 57 *"parallel play" experiences*: Kenneth H. Rubin, William Bukowski, and Jeffrey G. Parker, "Peer Interactions, Relationships, and Groups," in *Handbook of Child Psychology*, 5th ed., vol. 3, *Social, Emotional, and Personality Development*, ed. William Damon and Nancy Eisenberg (New York: Wiley, 1998), 589.

Page 59 *twice as much "private speech"*: Paige E. Davis, Elizabeth Meins, and Charles Fernyhough, "Individual Differences in Children's Private Speech: The Role of Imaginary Companions," *Journal of Experimental Child Psychology* 116, no. 3 (2013): 561–71.

Page 62 *Wonder Woman was created*: "Wonder Woman," Comic Vine, last modified March 6, 2014, www.comicvine.com/wonder-woman /4005-2048/.

Page 66 *more than half of U.S. schools*: Jay Mathews, "Children Learn Much from Field Trips That They Can't Get from Lectures or Textbooks," *Washington Post*, January 29, 2014, www.washingtonpost.com/lifestyle /on-parenting/children-learn-much-from-field-trips-that-they-cant -get-from-lectures-or-textbooks/2014/01/27/467d96b4-845a-11e3-bbe5 -6a2a3141e3a9_story.html.

Page 69 *"build it" in Swahili*: Catherine Chambers, *Swahili*, Languages of the World (Chicago: Heinemann First Library, 2012), 9.

Page 72 *During the 1953 coronation*: Marjorie Ingall, "The Woman behind the Dolls," *Tablet Magazine*, May 7, 2013, www.tabletmag.com/jewish -life-and-religion/131508/the-woman-behind-the-dolls.

Page 73 *"Finally, the outfit became ridiculous"*: Tama Kieves, *Inspired & Unstoppable: Wildly Succeeding in Your Life's Work!* (New York: Tarcher, 2013), 24.

Page 75 *The David Crowder Band*: Bruce Farr, "Tripping the Light Creative," *Prime Living*, November–December 2013, 16, http://issuu .com/srgpublications/docs/31_pl_nd13_lores/18?e=1274578/5392866.

Page 80 *a 1962 marketing campaign*: William H. Honan, "H.R. Ball, 79, Ad Executive Credited with Smiley Face," *New York Times*, April 14, 2001, www.nytimes.com/2001/04/14/us/h-r-ball-79-ad-executive-credited -with-smiley-face.html.

Page 83 *Hasbro gave a makeover*: Stacy Zeiger, "How the New Clue Board Game Differs from the Classic," LoveToKnow, accessed May 1, 2014, http://boardgames.lovetoknow.com/New_Clue_Board_Game.

Page 83 *"Useful Pot to put things in"*: A.A. Milne, *Winnie-the-Pooh* (London: Methuen Children's Books, 1992), 73.

Page 86 *The Treehotel in Sweden*: "About Us," Treehotel, accessed May 1, 2014, www.treehotel.se/?pg=about.

Page 86 *"Nothing is more intimate"*: Thomas Moore, *The Re-enchantment of Everyday Life* (New York: HarperCollins, 1996), 85.

Page 89 *the electronic memory game*: Benj Edwards, "Simon Turns 30," 1UP. com, accessed May 1, 2014, www.1up.com/features/simon-turns-30.

Page 90 *"When we treat children's play"*: Fred Rogers, *The World According to Mr. Rogers: Important Things to Remember* (New York: Hyperion Books, 2003), 183.

Page 92 *A 2009 study*: Singer et al., "Children's Pastimes."

Page 95 *Role play*: Thomas G. Power, *Play and Exploration in Children and Animals* (Mahwah, NJ: Lawrence Erlbaum, 2000), 393.

Page 99 *In the Disney animated film*: "The Jabberwocky," *Alice in Wonderland* wiki, accessed May 1, 2014, http://aliceinwonderland.wikia.com /wiki/The_Jabberwocky.

Page 105 *Fred A. Birchmore*: David V. Herlihy, *Bicycle: The History* (New Haven, CT: Yale University Press, 2004), 359–60.

Page 108 *The Spirograph toy*: Walsh, *Timeless Toys*, 208.

Page 111 *Ring pops*: Silvia Larin, "5 Simple Ways to 'Pop the Question' to Your Bridesmaids," Ethical Bride, July 21, 2013, www.ethicalbride .com/5-simple-ways-to-pop-the-question-to-your-bridesmaids/.

Page 114 *Etch A Sketch*: Walsh, *Timeless Toys*, 178.

Page 117 *originated Theatresports*: Jeanne Leep, *Theatrical Improvisation: Short Form, Long Form, and Sketch-Based Improv* (New York: Palgrave Macmillan, 2008), 25.

Page 121 *The Very Hungry Caterpillar*: "New Poll Celebrates the 45th Anniversary of the Very Hungry Caterpillar," The Joester Loria Group blog, March 25, 2014, http://joesterloriagroup.com/blog/new-poll -celebrates-45th-anniversary-hungry-caterpillar/.

Page 124 *Scrabble's most valuable eight-letter word*: Jennifer M. Wood, "10 Words That Will Win You Any Game of Scrabble," *Mental Floss*, April 13, 2013, http://mentalfloss.com/article/50090/10-words-will-win-you -any-game-scrabble.

Page 125 *positive interactions with* strangers: Elizabeth W. Dunn and
    Michael Norton, "Hello, Stranger," *New York Times*, April 25, 2014,
    www.nytimes.com/2014/04/26/opinion/sunday/hello-stranger
    .html?_r=0.

Page 134 *largest game of hide-and-seek*: "Largest Game of Hide-and-Seek,"
    Guinness World Records, accessed May 1, 2014, www.guinnessworld
    records.com/records-3000/largest-game-of-hide-and-seek/.

Page 137 *Artwiculate is a Twitter-based*: Barb Dybwad, "Artwiculate Turns
    Twitter Wordsmithing into a Game," Mashable, September 21, 2009,
    http://mashable.com/2009/09/21/artwiculate/.

Page 143 *The "stone" in a mood ring*: Anne Marie Helmenstine, "How
    Do Mood Rings Work?," About.com, accessed May 1, 2014,
    http://chemistry.about.com/od/chemistryfaqs/f/moodring.htm.

Page 146 *For the movie* WALL-E: Richard Siklos, "Apple and Eve,"
    CNNMoney, May 12, 2008, www.money.cnn.com/2008/05/09
    /technology/siklos_walle.fortune/.

Page 149 *Silly Putty*: Ed Sobey and Woody Sobey, *The Way Toys Work: The
    Science behind the Magic 8 Ball, Etch A Sketch, Boomerang, and More*
    (Chicago: Chicago Review Press, 2008), 126.

Page 153 *Guy Laliberté*: "About Cirque du Soleil," Cirque du Soleil, accessed
    May 1, 2014, www.cirquedusoleil.com/en/help/about/cirque-du-soleil
    .aspx.

Page 154 *"Space wasn't a problem"*: "History of the Circus," PBS, accessed
    May 1, 2014, www.pbs.org/opb/circus/in-the-ring/history-circus/.

Page 156 *"genuine American fortune cookies"*: Michael T. Kaufman, "A
    Fortune Will Greet You in an Endeavor Faraway," *New York Times*,
    November 7, 1992, www.nytimes.com/1992/11/07/nyregion/about-new
    -york-a-fortune-will-greet-you-in-an-endeavor-faraway.html.

Page 160 *Christian mystic Henry Suso*: Elisabeth Dutton, *Julian of Norwich:
    The Influence of Late-Medieval Devotional Compilations* (Cambridge,
    UK: Brewer, 2008), 90.

Page 160 *The Sanskrit word lila*: "Lila," *Encyclopaedia Britannica*, accessed
    May 1, 2014, www.britannica.com/EBchecked/topic/1549146/lila.

Page 162 *Rubik's Cube*: Solomon W. Golomb, "Rubik's Cube and Quarks,"
    American Scientist 7 (May–June 1982): 257–59.

Page 166 *Kermit the Frog*: Sara Franks-Allen, "10 Things You Didn't Know
    about Kermit the Frog," TheFW, September 24, 2013, http://thefw.com
    /things-you-didnt-know-about-kermit-the-frog/.

Page 169 *The Magic 8 Ball*: Walsh, *Timeless Toys*, 97.

Page 172 *sand gardens*: Playground and Recreation Association of America,
    "A Brief History of the Playground in America," *Playground* 9 (April
    1915): 2.

Page 173 *"Every thought and experience"*: "Chakras," Caroline Myss's web-site, accessed May 1, 2014, www.myss.com/library/chakras/.

Page 175 *Johnny Gruelle's original*: Patricia Hall, *Johnny Gruelle, Creator of Raggedy Ann and Andy* (Gretna, LA: Pelican, 1993), 111.

Page 178 *pre-1960 vintage carousels*: "Carousels with Awards and Special Features," National Carousel Association, accessed May 1, 2014, http://carousels.org/USACensus/stdqueries/census-awards.html.

Page 178 *electric-bolt effect*: Catherine Shoard, "The Wizard of Oz: 71 Facts for the Film's 71st Birthday," *Guardian*, August 12, 2010, www .theguardian.com/film/2010/aug/12/the-wizard-of-oz-google-doodle.

Page 182 *"Don't ask what the world"*: Walter Fluker, *Ethical Leadership: The Quest for Character, Civility, and Community* (Minneapolis: Fortress Press, 2009), 170.

Page 187 *Pixar movies contain*: Gregory Wakeman, "14 Toy Story Facts You Probably Didn't Know," *Andy's Toybox* (blog), December 9, 2013, https://uk.movies.yahoo.com/14-toy-story-facts-probably-didn-t -know-232900627.html.

Page 188 *"The more I want"*: Richard Bach, *Illusions: The Adventures of a Reluctant Messiah* (New York: Dell, 1977), 40.

Page 192 *from a quote by Francis Xavier*: Adam Taylor, "7 Observations from Watching an Epic Documentary on Modern Britain," Business Insider, November 12, 2013, www.businessinsider.com/seven-up-7 -observations-on-epic-documentary-series-2013-10.

Page 193 *"Law of Least Effort"*: Deepak Chopra, *The Seven Spiritual Laws of Success: A Practical Guide to the Fulfillment of Your Dreams* (San Rafael, CA: Amber-Allen, 1994), 30.

Page 195 *The original Kenner*: "Easy-Bake Oven," National Toy Hall of Fame, accessed May 1, 2014, www.toyhalloffame.org/toys/easy-bake -oven.

Page 200 *Minoru Wada*: Bernard Spodek and Olivia N. Saracho, eds., *International Perspectives on Research in Early Childhood Education* (Greenwich, CT: Information Age, 2005), 139.

Page 203 *Tinkertoys were invented*: "Fascinating Facts about the Invention of the Tinkertoy Construction Sets by Charles Pajeau in 1914," The Great Idea Finder, last modified March 2005, www.ideafinder.com /history/inventions/tinkertoy.htm.

Page 206 *Egyptian tomb drawings*: Charles Panati, *Extraordinary Origins of Everyday Things* (New York: Perennial Library, 1987), 370.

Page 207 *David Allen*: David Allen, *Getting Things Done: The Art of Stress-Free Productivity* (New York: Penguin Books, 2001), 22.

Page 210 *"If one advances"*: Henry David Thoreau, *Walden* (New York: Crowell, 1910), 427.

Page 213 *All twelve-inch G.I. Joe*: Walsh, *Timeless Toys*, 202.

Page 217 *I recommend the amazing work of Hal and Sidra Stone*: For more information about the work of Hal and Sidra Stone, see their website: www.voicedialogueinternational.com.

Page 220 *The game Truth or Dare*: Brian Grover, "Truth or Dare in Many Languages," Speekeezy blog, May 5, 2010, www.speekeezy.ca/blog /35-truth-or-dare/47-truth-or-dare-in-many-languages.html.

Page 223 *The Frisbee*: Sharon M. Scott, *Toys and American Culture: An Encyclopedia* (Santa Barbara, CA: ABC-CLIO, 2010), 117.

Page 226 *Lionel Trains*: Walsh, *Timeless Toys*, 9.

Page 226 *scene in* The Cat in the Hat: Dr. Seuss, *The Cat in the Hat* (New York: Random House, 1985), 58.

Page 228 *"We do a lot of looking"*: Frederick Franck, *The Zen of Seeing: Seeing/Drawing as Meditation* (New York: Vintage, 1973), 3.

Page 229 *The longest marathon*: "Most Bounces in a Pogo Stick Marathon (Male)," Guinness World Records, accessed May 1, 2014, www.guinness worldrecords.com/records-1/most-consecutive-pogo-stick-jumps -%28male%29.

Page 232 *An amazing 64 percent*: "Famous Formers," Girl Scouts of Greater Chicago and Northwest Indiana, accessed May 1, 2014, www.girl scoutsgcnwi.org/famous-formers.

Page 235 *the cuckoo clock was inspired*: "The History of the Cuckoo Clock," Black Forest Hill, accessed May 1, 2014, www.black-forest-hill.com.au /products/cuckoos/history.html.

Page 238 *In the Middle Ages*: "Born with a Silver Spoon in the Mouth…," MotherPie (blog), July 24, 2006, www.motherpie.typepad.com /motherpie/2006/07/born_with_a_sil.html.

Page 241 *first recognizable fire sprinkler*: "A History of Fire Sprinklers," Fire Safety Toolbox, accessed May 1, 2014, www.firesafetytoolbox.org.uk /history-fireSprinklers.html.

Page 241 *Water is used in play therapy*: Ken Schwartzenberger, "Experiential Play Therapy," Play Therapy Seminars, April 2004, www.play therapyseminars.com/Articles/Details/10001.

Page 244 *Piggy banks weren't always*: "Piggy Bank History," The Piggy Bank Page, accessed May 1, 2014, www.piggybankpage.co.uk/piggy _bank_history.htm.

Page 246 *Gumby wasn't originally*: "History," Gumby website, accessed May 1, 2014, www.gumbyworld.com/art-clokey-gumby-history/.

Page 247 *"Your whole heart"*: Robert Henri, *The Art Spirit* (New York: Basic Books, 2007), 123.

Page 249 *The Japanese company*: "A Brief Look at the Cymbal Banging Monkey Toy Charley Chimp's History," The Classic "Cymbal Banging

Monkey" Toy, accessed May 1, 2014, www.cymbalbangingmonkey
.com/history.html.

Page 252 *The Boston Marathon's*: John Forrester, "The History of the Boston Marathon Finish Line," Runner's World, April 16, 2014,
www.runnersworld.com/boston-marathon/the-history-of-the
-boston-marathon-finish-line.

Page 254 *Candy Land was invented*: Simara Kawash, "Polio Comes Home:
Pleasure and Paralysis in Candy Land," *Journal of Play* 3 (Fall 2010):
186.

Page 254 *the "Law of Giving"*: Chopra, *Seven Spiritual Laws*, 13.

Page 257 *In July 2013*: Courtney Subramanian, "WATCH: 272,297 Dominoes Fall for New World Record," *Time*, July 18, 2013, http://ncwsfccd
.time.com/2013/07/18/watch-272297-dominoes-fall-for-new-world
-record/.

Page 260 *Strawberry Shortcake*: Christopher Byrne, *Toy Time! From Hula
Hoops to He-Man to Hungry Hungry Hippos; A Look Back at the
Most-Beloved Toys of Decades Past* (New York: Three Rivers Press,
2013), 36.

Page 263 *The game of backgammon*: Chuck Bower, "History of Backgammon," Backgammon Galore!, accessed May 1, 2014, www.bkgm.com
/articles/GOL/Aug99/chuck.htm.

Page 264 *"How do geese know"*: Richard Worth, *Elisabeth Kübler-Ross:
Encountering Death and Dying* (New York: Chelsea House, 2005), 20.

Grown-Up Books about Play

A RECOMMENDED READING LIST

I t seems that kids don't write much about play — probably because they're doing it. But here are some very interesting *grown-up* books about the influences and effects of play, in case you're interested in further exploration. Note that every hour spent studying play theory is most effective when balanced by one hour of drawing with crayons, tossing a Frisbee, or dressing up in funny hats.

Cultural Observation and Study

Brown, Stuart. *Play: How It Shapes the Brain, Opens the Imagination, and Invigorates the Soul*. New York: Avery, 2009.
Kane, Pat. *The Play Ethic: A Manifesto for a Different Way of Living*. London: Pan Macmillan, 2004.
Power, Thomas G. *Play and Exploration in Children and Animals*. Mahwah, NJ: Lawrence Erlbaum, 2000.

Productivity and Creativity

Carroll, Kevin. *The Red Rubber Ball at Work: Elevate Your Game through the Hidden Power of Play*. New York: McGraw-Hill, 2008.
Csikszentmihalyi, Mihaly. *Finding Flow: The Psychology of Engagement with Everyday Life*. New York: Basic Books, 1997.
Pink, Daniel H. *A Whole New Mind: Why Right-Brainers Will Rule the Future*. New York: Riverhead Books, 2006.

Play in Child Development

Elkind, David. *The Power of Play: Learning What Comes Naturally.* Cambridge, MA: Da Capo Press, 2007.

Paley, Vivian Gussin. *A Child's Work: The Importance of Fantasy Play.* Chicago: University of Chicago Press, 2004.

Rogers, Fred. *The World According to Mr. Rogers: Important Things to Remember.* New York: Hyperion Books, 2003.

About the Author

Marney K. Makridakis is the founder of Artella Land, a groundbreaking online community for artists, writers, and creative individuals. Marney is a widely known voice in the creativity movement, frequently requested for interviews, guest columns, workshops, and speeches. She has created hundreds of online workshops and courses, and teaches virtual and in-person classes and workshops across the United States. Marney is publisher of *Artella* magazine, and bestselling author of *Creating Time: Using Creativity to Reinvent the Clock and Reclaim Your Life*.

Marney is also the originator of the ARTbundance approach to self-discovery through creativity and has trained over three hundred coaches and practitioners in the ARTbundance Certification Training program (ACT).

A graduate of Duke University, Marney playfully Hops, Skips, and Jumps in Denton, Texas, with her wonderful husband and their wise and adventurous young son, Kai. She considers the following things essential to her creative well-being: the color orange, poetic novels, singing loudly, daily naps, the love of a good man, and hero worship of Mary Poppins.

Pick up your free companion *Hop, Skip, Jump* Productivity Pack to supercharge this book! Playfully designed to help you manifest even faster, the Productivity Pack includes:

- The special report *The Three Biggest Things You Can Do to Change Work into Play* Today!
- The *Hop, Skip, Jump* emagazine — a full-color adventure of play, productivity, and passion
- The *Playful Prescription for Healthy Laughter* ebook, which contains bonus productivity lists to keep you chuckling
- A complete bundle of the printables referenced in this book
- Free Artella membership for bursts of creative inspiration

To download your free Productivity Pack, go to: www.ArtellaLand.com/hsj-downloads.html

About Artella Land

Get Inspired in the Enchanting Isles of Artella Land

"Marney Makridakis's Artella Land is a creative fountain; the site just vibrates with joyful creative expression."

– SARK

"I don't know why Artella hasn't been nominated for a Pulitzer yet. Seriously, Artella has changed the scope of art and words forever."

– Jill Badonsky

Visit Artella Land's supportive, inspiring community of writers, artists, crafters, entrepreneurs, and creative spirits! Artella Land is full of resources that offer an exciting map to creative inspiration and discovery, including:

* Monthly publications for Artella's ARTbundance and Business Bohemia adventures

- Hundreds of virtual programs, classes, and ebooks for creative spirits
- *Artella* magazine, the print magazine of words and art, where it all began
- The renowned ARTbundance Certification Training program
- Marney's Mapping and Mentoring Program for playful and profitable creative businesses

To visit Artella Land, go to:
www.ArtellaLand.com

Become an ARTbundance Coach or Practitioner

ARTbundance Certification Training (ACT) is a fourteen-week program that offers comprehensive training and turnkey materials for using the ARTbundance principles and ARTsignments in a variety of professional venues, including coaching, public speaking, teaching, leading workshops, and creating online learning environments.

ACT is a joyful, immensely gratifying opportunity for those who would like to use their deep interests and passion for creativity to serve and inspire others through creative, satisfying work.

If you are interested in learning how ACT can help you find and live your true creative calling, you can download a free ACT welcome pack, including:

- Free ARTbundance classes
- The Audio ACTimonials program, with real ACT graduates sharing their experiences
- The *Is ACT for Me?* workbook, with fun, innovative ARTsignments to help you determine if ACT might be the next step on your creative path

To download your free ACT welcome pack, go to:
www.ArtellaLand.com/ACT-pack.html